This book may be kept

CONSCIENCE
AND ITS RIGHT TO FREEDOM

CONSCIENCE
AND ITS
RIGHT TO
FREEDOM

ERIC D'ARCY

Lecturer in Philosophy in
the University of Melbourne

SHEED AND WARD—NEW YORK

MANUFACTURED IN THE UNITED STATES OF AMERICA

CONTENTS

PART II

THE BASIS OF THE ARGUMENT: THE AUTHORITY OF CONSCIENCE

PART III

THE BREAKDOWN OF THE ARGUMENT: ST. THOMAS ON RELIGIOUS FREEDOM

PART IV

A RECONSTRUCTION OF THE ARGUMENT: THE RIGHT TO FREEDOM OF CONSCIENCE

ABBREVIATIONS

PL   *Patrologia Latina*
PG   *Patrologia Graeca*
ST   *Summa Theologica*
AAS *Acta Apostolicae Sedis*

PREFACE

MANY arguments have been advanced in favour of the right to religious freedom, and this essay seeks to present a version of one of them: that based on the individual's duty to follow the dictates of his conscience. It studies St. Thomas Aquinas' account of the nature and authority of conscience, and some of the conclusions to which this theory seems to lead. Since the Thomist idiom and method are unfamiliar to many people, reference is made, from time to time, to British moralists, both classical and contemporary.

Two main conclusions are put forward. The first, which is arrived at in the second chapter, holds that a person is always morally obliged to follow a judgement of conscience formed in good faith. The second is argued from this, and reached in the final chapter. It claims that every adult has a strict right to religious freedom, and that the State is guilty of injustice if it interferes with a person's following his conscience in matters of religious choice, profession and worship. It is suggested that this right is satisfactorily recognized and protected in such documents as the constitutions of the Commonwealth of Australia, the Republic of Éire, and the United States of America.

I wish to acknowledge my indebtedness to a number of people who have helped me in the work. In the University of Melbourne, Dr. H. J. McCloskey and Dr. M. J. Charlesworth directed the basic research, and subjected the topic to exacting and fruitful examination at every stage. Professor A. Boyce Gibson rescued me from difficulties at two points in the final chapter, and advised me about preparing the essay for publication. In Oxford Mr. J. C. B. Gosling, Mr. P. T. Geach and Miss G. E. M. Anscombe each read the manuscript and made many valuable suggestions; and I profited greatly from discussions with Professor Gilbert Ryle, Professor H. L. A. Hart and Mrs. P. R. Foot, and with Professor R. D. Brandt during his visit from Swarthmore College, Pennsylvania.

My thanks are due in particular to Monsignor James Bourke, of the Archdiocese of Perth; his detailed criticism of the manuscript saved me from many inelegancies and mistakes. I also learnt a great deal from discussions with Father Vincent Turner, of Campion Hall, Oxford, Father Anthony Kenny, of the Archdiocese of Liverpool, Father John Burnheim, of the Archdiocese of Sydney, and Father Leo Kelly, of my own archdiocese, Melbourne.

Apart from the scriptural passages, I have made my own translations, except where acknowledged in the text.

PART I

THE TERMS OF THE ARGUMENT
CONSCIENCE AND SYNDERESIS

ONE of the principal tasks of this essay is to argue that a person is always bound to follow the dictates of conscience formed in good faith. The arguments which will be here advanced in favour of this thesis are largely derived from those of St. Thomas Aquinas. To follow his case satisfactorily, however, it is necessary first to examine what he means by the term *conscience*. A warning about his theory might be sounded in the words of a contemporary Oxford moral philosopher; Mr. Hare writes:

> We must not think that if we can decide between one course and another without further thought (it seems self-evident to us, which we should do), this necessarily implies that we have some mysterious intuitive faculty which tells us what to do.[1]

Conscience has often been taken for a special faculty, or a moral sense, or a voice within the soul; but for St. Thomas, as for Hare, it is none

[1] R. M. Hare, *The Language of Morals*, Oxford, Clarendon Press, 1952, p. 64.

of these things. In this chapter, therefore, we shall investigate the meaning and application of the term "conscience" in St. Thomas' writings, leaving until the next chapter a study of the moral authority with which he credits it.

This calls first for a brief historical sketch of his data. The scholastics inherited four lines of thought on the subject of conscience, and these provided the raw materials for the medieval debates on the topic.

1. THE HISTORICAL SOURCES

In English we have done with the Latin word *conscientia* what neither Latin nor French has done; we have, as Rickaby says, "doubled" the term, reserving "conscience" for the moral department, and devising "consciousness" for use in the non-moral field of "awareness". In Greek, as in Latin and French, a single word serves both purposes; one is left to decide from the context whether or not in a given place it has a moral connotation.

In moral discourse the English word "conscience" itself has a dual role. The first refers to a familiar experience, that of looking back and pronouncing judgement on one's past moral performance; this we shall call "judicial conscience". The second refers to the cases where, confronted by the need to make a moral choice or decision, we say that conscience lays down or dictates what should be done; this we shall call "legislative conscience". In the writings of moralists before St. Paul, only the first is found.

1. THE PAGAN USAGE: JUDICIAL CONSCIENCE

The Greek word for conscience, συνείδησις, first occurs in a fragment of Democritus.[1] Many scholars, though not all, credit it here with a distinctly moral significance, and would render it somewhat as follows:

> There are men who are quite ignorant of what is to follow the dissolution of their mortal nature; yet, because their conscience is burdened with the memory of their evil conduct, they torment themselves, all their lives long, by inventing myths and fables about a life after death.

If this interpretation is correct, then, conscience first appears in the guise of remorse.

According to Ast,[2] the noun συνείδησις does not occur in Plato. However, the verb συνειδέναι is found nineteen times. Of these only one seems to have a moral flavour: in the *Symposium*, Alcibiades says, "Socrates makes me conscious

[1] H. Diels, *Die Fragmente der Vorsokratiker*, Berlin, Wiedmannsche, 1951, 68, B 297.
[2] D. F. Ast, *Lexicon Platonicum*, Berlin, Barsdorf, 1908, vol. 3, p. 323.

that I cannot deny the duty of doing his bidding."[1] In one other place, strangely not listed by Ast, the verb clearly bears a moral connotation. In the *Republic*, Cephalus says, "The man who is conscious of no wrong looks forward with cheerfulness and hope."[2]

Aristotle did not use the noun συνείδησις, and according to Deman[3] it is not found again in its moral usage until just before the Christian era. He quotes Denys of Halicarnassus, Diodorus of Sicily, Philo and Josephus, finding that with all of them it (or frequently the neuter participle, τὸ συνειδός) is a "guilty conscience" evoked by some evil deed; it is something painful and distressing. There is no trace of any function attributed to conscience *before* morally responsible action.

The corresponding Latin word is *conscientia*, and its use is much more common than συνείδησις in Greek. As with the Greek, it is by no means confined to moral usage; indeed, this is the last sense given it by Lewis and Short. They give:

Conscientia. I. A joint knowledge of something, a being privy to, a knowing along with

[1] 216 b.

[2] 331 a, trans. H. D. P. Lee, Penguin, 1955.

[3] H. Deman, in *Traduction française de la Somme théologique: La Prudence*, Paris, Desclée, 1932, p. 480. The present summary is indebted to his "Renseignements techniques".

others . . . II. Consciousness, knowledge, feeling, sense; in particular, a consciousness of right and wrong, the moral sense, conscience.

This usage is extensive in Cicero and Seneca; but still we find the function of conscience as judicial only. It looks back on the life we have led or the deed we have done, and it pronounces judgement; and that judgement cannot be gainsaid or overruled by other people's opinion of us, good or ill. Cicero says:

I do not set much store by what others think of me; my own conscience counts for more with me than the verdict of all other people.[1]

Nor is this judgement merely speculative: in the light of its verdict it rewards or punishes a man in a peculiarly interior and effective way. Thus Cicero echoes the words of Cephalus in the *Republic*:

The consciousness of a life well led, the memory of many deeds well done—this is a blessed thing.[2]

The evil man has a conscience too; it knows his wrongdoing and condemns it, and torments him with its memory; his sin is ever before him, and nothing can raze out the written troubles of the

[1] *Ad Att.* XII, 28.
[2] *De Senectute*, 3,9.

brain; interior suffering is the natural consequence of sin. Seneca writes:

A good conscience enlists a multitude of
friends; a bad conscience is distressed and
anxious, even when alone.[1]

So we find in pre-Christian writers what we
have called judicial conscience. After an action
is performed conscience passes moral judgement
upon it. Other judges may be venal or partial
or fallible; not so the verdict of conscience. If
its verdict is favourable, peace of soul is our
reward; if unfavourable, we suffer the pangs of
remorse. The mind is its own place.

2. ST. PAUL'S INNOVATION: LEGISLATIVE
CONSCIENCE

St. Paul found it convenient to use the word
"conscience" in an entirely new sense, but he
did not abandon the old one. The term occurs
twenty-three times in his epistles, and in fifteen
of these it has the meaning and function which
it had in the pagan writers: an interior witness
and judge of one's past actions and motives,
which can be a source of comfort or of remorse.
This must not be exaggerated. St. Paul did not
encourage complacency or self-righteousness in
the name of conscience: "My conscience does
not, in fact, reproach me, but that is not where

[1] *Ep.*, 43,5.

my justification lies; it is the Lord's scrutiny I must undergo";[1] Christ is our only final judge. But the concept is recognized and used.

In eight places, however, we encounter something quite new. In the First Epistle to the Corinthians, the problems of certain individuals' scruples concerning the right course of action leads St. Paul to use the phrase, "Their conscience is uneasy, doubtful";[2] the context shows that this defective condition is the product, not only of timidity, but of ignorance too. Being a conscience, it imposes a rule of conduct; yet for all that it may be mistaken. Here then are two new features in the use of the word "conscience": that of having authority to legislate; and that of being subject to error.

The discussion arises when St. Paul takes up the problem of eating meat bought in the open market after it has been used in idolatrous worship. Really, he says, there is no objection to this at all; still, there are some who feel that eating such meat identifies them with the pagan rites. Ronald Knox suggests that they may have been heathens feeling the attraction of the new faith, or Jewish Christians who still felt themselves bound by the rule laid down at the Council of Jerusalem. Whoever they were, they laboured under a false conscience on the issue, and the

[1] 1 Cor. 4.4.
[2] 1 Cor. 8.7,10,12.

gist of St. Paul's advice is that a man must not act against his conscience. Knox comments:

> The principle, in either case, is that a man is bound to follow his own conscience, and we must sometimes abstain from what our own conscience finds harmless, lest our example should give scandal to one whose conscience is differently formed.[1]

Two chapters later, St. Paul takes up a related question: If invited to dine with a pagan friend, may a Christian eat meat that has been used in idolatrous worship? His solution bears directly on the topic of this essay; indeed, if this were a study of the problem of religious freedom in Scripture, it could serve as an excellent starting-point. He coins and three times uses a phrase which the Douai (Catholic) and Authorized (Anglican) translations have made classical in the form "for conscience' sake". Knox renders the passage as follows:

> When things are sold in the open market, then you may eat, without making any enquiries to satisfy your consciences; this world, as we know, and all that is in it belongs to the Lord. If some unbeliever invites you to his table, and you consent to go, then you need not ask questions to satisfy your consciences, you may eat whatever is put before you. But

[1] Footnote to *v.* 7.

if someone says to you, this has been used in idolatrous worship, then for the sake of your informant you must refuse to eat; it is a matter of conscience; his conscience, I mean, not yours.[1]

This makes St. Paul's answer quite clear. The reason for his answer, given in the next sentences, is not so clear, and Knox suggests a probable paraphrase:

Keep your own interior liberty of conscience, although you abstain out of charity; one man's conscience cannot be the rule for another's.[2]

The new usage of the word "conscience" occurs also in the Epistle to the Romans. Here St. Paul uses it to stress the point that obedience to civil authority is not a matter of mere expediency, but a full-blooded moral obligation.

Thou must needs, then, be submissive, not only for fear of punishment, but in conscience.[3]

St. Paul, then, introduces an entirely new phase in the history of the term "conscience" in moral theory, and two new features characterize his use of it. First, it is to play a *directive* role *before* action takes place. In the pagan writers conscience did not appear on the scene until

[1] 1 Cor. 10.25–9.
[2] Footnote to *vv*. 29–30.
[3] Rom. 13.5.

after the action was performed, and its role was purely *judicial*; but in St. Paul, conscience is credited with a legislative function, and it induces an obligation in the proper sense. Second, conscience is fallible: the directions it issues may be mistaken; but whether it be mistaken or not, it seems that we are bound to follow its rulings.

3. The Fathers: Both Usages Adopted

The bridge between St. Paul and the scholastics is made, of course, by the Fathers of the Church. A technical term used twenty-three times in the Pauline epistles was assured of a place in Christian moral writing. For the Fathers, both Greek and Latin, conscience was a familiar, though not a well-developed, concept, both in its judicial and its legislative roles. Our interest lies in those writings which shaped Aquinas' views on conscience; let us notice, then, the chief patristic elements that he himself quotes.

First, from St. Ambrose. Given his career in the imperial service and his late conversion to Christianity, it is no surprise to find in him more sometimes of Cicero and Seneca than of St. Paul; indeed, his *De Officiis* not merely borrows Cicero's title, but also has been thought by some scholars to imitate his style. St. Thomas was to draw on that work to illustrate judicial conscience. For Ambrose, conscience is the interior judge, infallible and majestic, whose sanction none can escape. We should measure a man's fortune, he says,

> ... according to the state of his conscience within him. That is an accurate and incorruptible judge of innocence and guilt.[1]

From St. Basil, the scholastics took over the phrase which they rendered *naturale judicatorium*. St. Thomas himself quotes the phrase in the *De Veritate* and in the *Summa Theologica*. We might have expected the scholastics to associate the phrase with judicial conscience, with the act of passing judgement on a deed already done; the Greek sometimes has the sense of a tribunal, and the Latin rendering suggests a judicial act. But they did not; they understood it as a natural power of distinguishing right from wrong, and so connected it with legislative conscience. It is in this way that the *Summa* connects the phrase with conscience, a term which Basil himself does not explicitly use. His passage reads:

> We have within us a natural power of judgement which enables us to distinguish right from wrong. So, when we are called on to choose what we shall do from several alterna-

[1] *De Officiis*, 1,12. (*PL*, 16,40.)

tives, we must exercise that power of judgement responsibly, like a judge who deliberates with impartiality and scrupulous honesty, upholding virtue and condemning vice.[1]

Yet there is a passage, more than a century earlier than Basil or Ambrose, which explicitly uses the word "conscience", and recognizes both its functions, the legislative and the judicial. It occurs in Origen's discussion of the famous verses,

As for the Gentiles, though they have no law to guide them, there are times when they carry out the precepts of the law unbidden, finding in their own natures a rule to guide them, in default of any other rule; and this shows that the obligations of the law are written in their hearts; their conscience utters its own testimony, and when they dispute with one another they find themselves condemning this, approving that.[2]

St. Thomas refers to Origen's treatment of this in each of his three main studies of the nature and function of conscience. He never quotes the text in full, but gives his own paraphrase. Origen actually says:

[1] *In Princ. Proverb.*, PG, 31,405–6.
[2] Rom. 2.14–15.

> I would hold that *conscience* is that spirit which, the Apostle says, is found in the soul as tutor, companion and guide. Its function is to advise one about the best course of action, and to rebuke and chastise one for sin.[1]

Here we have the word "conscience" itself, and we have the two functions of guiding and advising (legislative conscience), and of judging and punishing (judicial conscience).

St. John Damascene provided one other phrase for the scholastics; it is "the law of our mind".

> God's law enters our mind and draws it to itself by stirring up conscience, which itself is called the law of our mind.[2]

4. St. Jerome's Gloss: "Synderesis"

There, then, was the raw material for the medieval treatise on conscience. The ancient philosophers and St. Paul had put forward the two basic elements; the Fathers had indicated four or five main lines for development. The scholastics were familiar with all these passages, and needed only to elaborate them systematically for a full and clear rationale of conscience to emerge. Had this been the whole of the patristic data, the evolution might have been straightforward and smooth.

[1] *PG*, 14,893.
[2] *De Fide Orthodoxa*, 4,22. (*PG*, 94,1199.)

But a passage in St. Jerome cut right across the brief though consistent accounts of the other Fathers. It confused the whole matter with a new term and a new metaphor. And it was Jerome's gloss, rather than the passages we have already noticed, that dominated the scholastic studies up to and including the early work of St. Thomas. It determined the whole shape of the medieval treatises on conscience, so we must quote it in full.

It occurs in Jerome's commentary on the prophecy of Ezechiel. He is discussing the prophet's vision of the four living beings—a man, a lion, an ox, and an eagle.[1] He mentions several interpretations of the vision, and then rehearses one put forward by a number of "Platonizers". The key passage is as follows.[2]

These writers interpret the vision in terms of Plato's theory of the three elements of the soul. There are Reason, Spirit, and Desire; to these correspond respectively the man, the lion, and the ox. Now, above these three was the eagle; so in the soul, they say, above the other three elements and beyond them is a fourth, which the Greeks call *synderesis*. This is that spark of conscience which was not quenched even in the heart of Cain, when

[1] Ch. 1, especially verses 5–14.
[2] *Commentarium in Ezechielem*, 1,1. (*PL*, 25,22.)

he was driven out of paradise.[1] This it is that makes us, too, feel our sinfulness when we are overcome by evil Desire or unbridled Spirit, or deceived by sham Reason. It is natural to identify synderesis with the eagle, since it is distinct from the other three elements and corrects them when they err. This is that spirit which, as we read in Scripture, "intercedes for us with groans beyond all utterance".[2] "Who else can know a man's thoughts, except the man's own spirit that is within him?"[3] This is that spirit which Paul prayed might be kept unimpaired with soul and body.[4] And yet in some men we see this conscience overthrown and displaced; they have no sense of guilt or shame for their sins; as it is written, "Little the godless man recks of it, when he falls into sin's mire."[5] They deserve the rebuke, "Still never a blush on thy harlot's brow."[6]

There is some disagreement over the spelling of the new term, "synderesis" or "synteresis". There is controversy, too, concerning the word's origin. Some would derive it from συντηρεω, "I contemplate",[7] others suggest that a scribe has

[1] Gen. 4.13. [2] Rom. 8.26. [3] 1 Cor. 2.11.
[4] 1 Thess. 5.23. [5] Prov. 18.3. [6] Jer. 3.3.
[7] e.g., E. Genicot, *Institutiones Theologiae Moralis*, Brussels, Desclée, 1931, vol. 1, p. 41.

miscopied συνειδησις[1]. But textual points need not delay us; our only interest in the passage is its part in shaping the Thomist theory of conscience.

Had the medieval work on conscience simply developed the remarks of Origen, Basil and Damascene, then all might have been well. But about the year 1152 Peter the Lombard referred to this passage in Jerome,[2] and the mould of a century's debate was cast. Subsequent commentators turned up the passage, scrutinized it narrowly, and dealt with the subject of conscience and the sources of moral obligation in the terms it suggested; it was for them a point of departure, in the nature of their "Prolegomena to Any Future Ethics". A brief study of the text will show the problems and paradoxes it presents.

First comes a group of questions concerning this new term "synderesis". What is its essential nature? Jerome puts it on a footing with reason, spirit and desire, and for the scholastics these suggest the faculties of reason, irascible appetite, and concupiscible appetite. Is synderesis, then, a faculty?

If it is, has it kinship with intellect or will? Or, in scholastic terms, is it a faculty of the

---

[1] e.g., M. Prümmer, *Manuale Theologiae Moralis*, Fribourg, Herder, 1958, vol. 1, p. 197, *n.* 3.

[2] *Liber IV Sententiarum*, lib. 2, Dist. 39.

cognitive order or of the affective? Apparently
of the cognitive, for it is a spirit which "can
know a man's thoughts"; but on the other hand,
apparently of the affective, for it "makes us *feel*
our sinfulness". Again, can it be lost? Apparently it can, for some men "have no sense of
guilt or shame over their sins"; but on the
other hand, its spark "was not quenched even
in the heart of Cain".

Next, what is the relationship of this new
concept, synderesis, to conscience? Are they
two things, or are they one and the same? Apparently they are two, for synderesis seems to
be a spark from conscience's flame; yet the
phrase in the penultimate sentence, "this same
conscience", seems to identify them.

Finally, the passage prompts the same questions with regard to conscience that it did concerning synderesis. Is it a faculty? Has it kinship
with intellect or will? What is its function? Can
it be lost?

2. CONSCIENCE IN THE SCHOLASTICS

SUCH were the terms of reference for an inquiry that lasted a century. When Aquinas came to write on the subject of conscience he was entering this debate. His final position was very much his own, but the shape of his treatment was largely determined by the discussions which preceded it. We shall appreciate his own account much better if we know something of the context in which he was writing and the views he was meaning to reject. "On pense toujours contre quelqu'un."

1. SCHOLASTICS BEFORE ST. THOMAS

The questions we have anticipated were the questions St. Jerome's "gloss" ultimately provoked, and we can see that this would have been a logical order for taking them. But historically there was no such systematic pattern.[1] First came four decades of muddled, uncritical exegesis of the passage; three quotations will suffice to show what confusion prevailed.

---

[1] All the sources of the debate have been marshalled and reproduced in full in Dom. O. Lottin, *Psychologie et morale aux 12ᵉ et 13ᵉ siècles*, Louvain, 1948, vol. 2, pp. 103–350. The following summary, which is sufficient for our purpose, is greatly indebted to this work.

Somewhere between the years 1160 and 1165 Master Udo wrote the first of the many commentaries on the Sentences of Peter the Lombard. In it he identifies synderesis with reason:

> The eagle refers to synderesis, which is that higher reason which even in Cain was not extinguished. It is distinct from the other three [elements of the soul] and corrects them when they err.[1]

One cannot but remark on the cheerful insouciance of a writer who identifies synderesis with reason, and supports his view with a phrase which says that they are distinct, and indeed that one corrects the other.

Second, Simon of Bisiniano, a canonist writing about the year 1175, identifies synderesis as natural law:

> It would seem that natural law is the higher part of the soul, namely reason under the aspect which is called synderesis, which Scripture tells us could not be extinguished even in Cain.[2]

Third, Peter of Poitiers, in a book published in 1179, sees it as reason in the act of inclining man towards good or repelling him from evil:

[1] From Master Udo's *Quaestiones*, quoted by Lottin, p. 107.
[2] Quoted Lottin, p. 74.

Reason always resists evil and argues against it, and insists that it should not be done. There is no man so bad that reason does not rebuke his conscience, branding some things as evil. This is that spark of reason which could not be quenched even in Cain; the Greeks call it synderesis.[1]

Such quotations seem to indicate that the authority of the gloss was accepted without any sustained attempt to determine its meaning, let alone to test its validity. But from the turn of the century, in fifty or sixty years' copious writing on the subject, we can single out three decisive steps. First, Stephen Langton undertook a speculative analysis of synderesis (he had nothing to contribute on conscience); then Philip the Chancellor dealt with synderesis and conscience together in a single treatise; finally came St. Albert the Great's chapter on the two in his *Summa de Homine*.

(i) STEPHEN LANGTON

The first systematic study of the question was undertaken by Stephen Langton, who broached it about the year 1205 in the course of his study of free will. He made one contribution of capital importance, which was permanently accepted in Thomist moral theory: synderesis is concerned

[1] *Sententiarum Libri V*, 2,21, quoted Lottin, p. 109.

with moral judgements at the level of very general principles.

There are three faculties with a part to play in our moral life, he says: the lower appetite, reason, and synderesis. The lower appetite moves the reason towards evil, synderesis inclines it towards good; reason presides over them as a judge over two barristers.

This hint is amplified slightly in a question explicitly devoted to synderesis; it is "a power, a part of the power of reason, by which a man naturally hates what is evil."[1] This is just what we want to see elaborated: is it really a separate faculty, *vis*, or just an aspect of reason itself? But instead of examining the nature of synderesis, Langton becomes engrossed in two of its properties: Can it be extinguished? Is it capable of merit or demerit? One point in the latter question, remarked almost casually, is of lasting importance. He holds that synderesis cannot merit, and to a series of objections[2] the gist of his answer is this: Remorse of conscience is the work, not of synderesis, but of reason, for synderesis remains at the level of general principles, whereas reason descends to the concrete case; but it is precisely over the concrete case that remorse of conscience is felt; hence it is by

[1] Par. 1 of the Cambridge text quoted by Lottin, p. 112.

[2] Listed in full text, Lottin, pp. 112–14.

reason, and not by synderesis, that we sin. As for Jerome's phrase, "in some men we see this conscience overthrown and displaced", this simply means that, in spite of the protests of synderesis, the act it condemns is performed none the less.

So three points are beginning to emerge. First, synderesis is a faculty, though this is not held universally. Second, it belongs to the rational, and therefore cognitive, order; though it strives to turn man from evil will. Third, and by far most important, "Synderesis remains at the level of general principles, and does not descend to specific questions."[1]

Godfrey of Poitiers in the main follows his master Langton, but parts company with him on one interesting point: synderesis, he holds, can err. Many people have fallen into error on articles of faith such as the Holy Trinity; yet such doctrinal matters are known precisely by synderesis, and by it alone.

Synderesis is certainly fallible, since there are some truths concerning the Trinity which can be arrived at only by synderesis. Yet in these matters man is capable of error. Therefore synderesis can err.[2]

It is surprising to find the claim that revealed truths can be known by synderesis. It was widely

[1] Lottin, pp. 112–14, reply to the fourth objection.
[2] Reply to the fifteenth objection: quoted in Lottin, pp. 116–19.

agreed that synderesis was part of man's *natural* endowment; but revealed truths belonged to the *supernatural* order, and were inaccessible to man unless God chose to reveal them: "No one else can know God's thoughts but the Spirit of God."[1] The sharp distinction of the natural and the supernatural at the ontological level was not yet clearly worked out; but at the epistemological level, the distinction between truths accessible to the unaided reason, and truths that could be known only if revealed, was well recognized. Perhaps it had been overlooked by Godfrey. Perhaps he was breaking with the common view of synderesis as part of the natural equipment of man. Perhaps he had not thought the issue through at all.

(ii) PHILIP THE CHANCELLOR

So far there had been little interest in conscience. Attention had been focused rather on synderesis, and on its qualities rather than on its essential nature. The great Secular master, Philip the Chancellor, addressed himself to these questions in a formal treatise on synderesis and conscience about the year 1233. For us, two of his contributions are of real importance. First, on the nature of synderesis, he held that it was a *potentia habitualis*, a habit-like faculty. Second,

[1] 1 Cor. 2.11.

on the relationship of conscience and synderesis, he held that synderesis provides the major of a practical syllogism and that a judgement of conscience is the conclusion that results from combining this major with a minor premise provided by reason.

Philip is strongly drawn to the view that synderesis is a *habitus*, a moral habit. Concupiscence is a habit, distinct from the soul and its faculties, drawing us towards evil; so there must be another habit, distinct from the soul and its faculties, drawing us towards good. Further, the light is distinct from the faculty of sight that it enlightens; so, too, must synderesis be from the mental faculty that it enlightens. However, the authority of Jerome is too strong; so Philip compromises, and coins the puzzling phrase "habit-like faculty".

On the question, "Is synderesis a faculty or a habit?" I take the middle course: it is a habit-like faculty. In this way we can reconcile arguments that seem to be opposed. Scriptural arguments[1] persuade us that it is a faculty; the parallel with concupiscence suggests that it is a habit. We are led to the middle course, then: it is a habit-like faculty.[2]

[1] He mentions Ezech. 1, Mal. 2, and 1 Cor. 2.
[2] Quoted from Philip's treatise on synderesis, Lottin, pp. 140–42.

This seems simply to be throwing up one's hands in despair. The argument leads one to say that synderesis is a *habitus*, a disposition or special aspect of the reason; but the ancient authority shows it to be a separate faculty or power, *potentia*, quite distinct from the faculty of reason; very well, then, we shall merge the two and call it a habit-like faculty.[1] However, disappointing though this be, it is at least some preparation for a break with the tradition.

Philip shows more independence when he takes up the question, "Is synderesis a faculty of the cognitive order or of the appetitive?" that is, "Is it connected with discernment and judgement, or with willing and decision?" He firmly locates it in the appetitive order, though at the level of "rational, not sense-, appetite"; that is, it has to do with the desires that spring from the spiritual, rational side of human nature, and not with the desires or "drives" which spring from the animal side. It is the last vestige of "original justice" left to us after the fall. So many factors hinder our ascent to the sovereign good, but synderesis is one element in us that does battle against them. The natural will is

[1] This is my attempt to render Philip's *potentia habitualis*. Lottin softens the startling sound of this by translating it, in his French commentary, as "faculté doublé d'habitus", "a faculty combined with a habit".

drawn towards goodness of all kinds, and synderesis directs it towards moral goodness.[1]

Philip's work is important on another score;
he makes the first study of conscience. A list of
questions prompted by Jerome's famous gloss
has already been suggested. From Peter the
Lombard's reference to it in 1152 to Philip's
Summa, which appeared about 1230, attention
had been focused on the first group of questions,
those concerning synderesis. Philip is the first to
take up the next group: What is the relationship
between synderesis and conscience? Are they
distinct or identical? His answer is that conscience is not synderesis, but the result of applying synderesis to a datum of reason.

He gives a striking example. Synderesis provides the principle: It is a capital offence falsely
to claim to be the Son of God. Then comes the
datum of reason: Christ falsely claimed to be
the Son of God. The consequence of these is the
verdict of conscience: Christ should be put to
death. Conscience reaches an erroneous conclusion, not through any mistake of synderesis,
for its principle (he thinks) is quite true: but
through an error of reason which judged Christ's
claim to be false.

The result of Philip's work was that, from
about the year 1230, studies of moral theology

[1] The argument is reproduced in full by Lottin,
pp. 143–8.

had to present treatises that gave a single account of synderesis and conscience. The first ones were full of confusions and inconsistencies. Synderesis and conscience are seen sometimes as identical, sometimes as separate faculties, sometimes as faculty and habit, sometimes as faculty and art. By some writers synderesis is presented as inclining the *will* towards good, and conscience as inclining the *reason*. These gradually hardened into two schools, the voluntarism of the Franciscans and the intellectualism of the Dominicans. We may complete our sketch of the raw material of St. Thomas' work by reviewing the salient features of St. Bonaventure's and St. Albert's theories.

(iii) THE FRIARS

Philip was amongst the greatest of the Secular masters, who, together with the old orders, had dominated the intellectual life of the early Middle Ages. The Franciscans and the Dominicans, founded in the first quarter of the thirteenth century, were playing an increasingly prominent part by the middle of the 1230's. Having fought hard for ecclesiastical leave to teach in the great universities, they were beginning to justify their admission on the grounds of academic stature. At Paris, the Franciscans John de la Rochelle and Alexander of Hales, and the Dominican Roland of Cremona, had each produced a *summa* by the end of the decade. St. Bonaventure was to be the greatest of the Franciscan scholars of the thirteenth century, and among the Dominicans, St. Albert the Great ranks only below St. Thomas. Each addressed himself to the problem of conscience and synderesis in the terms of St. Jerome's gloss and on the lines of the questions it had raised for earlier exegetes.

Let us put Bonaventure's view in this way. Both reason and will have a part to play in our moral life, and each of them needs to be given some direction or inclination towards moral goodness. Conscience does this for the reason; synderesis does it for the will, where it resides as a "natural bias" inclining the will towards moral goodness, as indeed dispositions do incline the faculty where they reside to elicit acts of certain kind. "Synderesis is that which impels a man towards the good; and so it belongs to the affective order".[1]

Everything is ready for a statement that synderesis is an innate habit of the will, but once again the authority of Jerome proves too strong, and Bonaventure hesitates and finally compromises in the phrase of Philip. Like Philip, Bonaventure concludes, "Synderesis should be called a habit-like faculty rather than a habit."

[1] *Commentary on the Sentences*, 2, dist. 39, art. 1, q. 1 in med.

We are still left to wonder rather despairingly just what a "habit-like faculty" might be.

Albert the Great also finds the authority of Jerome's gloss too strong to shrug off, and also concludes by describing synderesis as "a habit-like faculty". But this seems a small concession to tradition when we see the new ground he broke. Synderesis is not to be connected with will, but with reason, and with practical reason at that. Just as the speculative reason can distinguish truth from falsehood by its mastery of self-evident principles, so the practical reason can distinguish good from evil by its grasp of the elementary moral principles—"Killing is wrong", "We should pity the afflicted", and so on; hence:

> Synderesis is a special faculty of the soul in which the universals of morality are written.[1]

So on the strength of Jerome's authority Albert and Bonaventure agree in holding that synderesis is a faculty (of some sort). By dint of personal conviction, they agree in holding that it produces in the soul an inclination towards moral goodness. They differ in their account of this, whether it be an inclination of the will, or an innate intellectual grasp of the first moral principles.

Finally, what were the views of the two Friar

[1] *Summa de Creaturis*, written *c.* 1132: q. 71, art. 1.

Doctors concerning conscience? Both agree on its connection with the practical reason in its function of making moral judgements, and both agree that it is not a faculty. There was nothing in Jerome to prejudice their studies here; they could go where the argument led them.

Bonaventure remarks[1] that in the language of the day the word "conscience" referred sometimes to a faculty, sometimes to a habit, sometimes to the object about which a moral judgement is made. The second of these usages, he says, is the proper one. Examining it more closely, Bonaventure held that this was a habit which belonged to the practical reason, and was partly acquired and partly innate. It was acquired in so far as the terms of the basic moral principles come to us through experience, but innate in so far as, once these are given, conscience immediately sees their evident and necessary connection. It was acquired, furthermore, in so far as the principles and judgements which follow from the primary principles cannot be immediately evident, since they are the product of deduction and application. Hence Bonaventure looks on conscience as providing the direction for all our moral life. It applies to all moral judgements, both universal principles and particular conclusions.

On this, Albert's disagreement is clear and

[1] *Commentary*, 2, dist. 39, art. 1, q. 2.

firm. Synderesis gives the universal principles; conscience is the judgement about the particular case. The judgement of conscience is, in fact, the conclusion of a syllogism, whose major is given by synderesis and whose minor is a datum of reason or sense-experience.

> I hold that conscience is the conclusion reached by practical reason from two premises. The major of the syllogism is given by synderesis, which inclines us towards goodness by providing us with the general principles of goodness. The minor is given by reason, which applies the particular to the universal. The conclusion thus reached is conscience.[1]

St. Albert's later *Commentary on the Sentences* adds nothing to this position, but merely presents it again as he discusses the Lombard's remarks about Jerome's gloss.

2. ST. THOMAS

It was in the context of this long-standing debate that St. Thomas addressed himself to the subject of conscience. In his early accounts, in his own *Commentary on the Sentences*, and in the *De Veritate*, it is clear that the argument inclines him to abandon the view that synderesis

[1] *Summa de Creaturis*, q. 72, art. 1.

is a faculty, but for him, too, the authority of Jerome proves too much. Later, however, in his most mature work, the *Summa Theologica*, his view is unambiguously his own. On the question of synderesis, he sets down his final position on its terminology, nature and function without allowing St. Jerome to sway him at all. On the question of conscience, he follows in the main the views of his master Albert, but also introduces some valuable refinements.

It will be as well to say something about the difficulty of translating St. Thomas' *habitus*. Its meaning is akin, not to the modern English "habit", but to Aristotle's ἕξις; and translators have never been happy about that. Ross mostly renders it as "state"—state of soul, state of mind, state of character; Edghill as "habit"; Thomson as "disposition".

It has been suggested[1] that, in many contexts, the nearest English equivalent is "skill"; the more so since Wittgenstein seems to have restored the status of knowledge, understanding, and the like, as abiding skills rather than as transient events or experiences; for instance:

In the sense in which there are processes (including mental processes) which are characteristic of understanding, understanding is not a mental process.

[1] By Father Anthony Kenny, in private conversation.

To understand a language, to know how to speak it—these are just the sort of thing St. Thomas means by *habitus*; "skill" or "ability" would do for them rather nicely. Furthermore, "skill" conveys the note of, not bare capability, but facility and readiness in performance which the term contains.

But in the present context it will not quite do. "Skill" often suggests a knack that I have acquired by practice, by the repetition of like actions; whereas the very *habitus* we have to discuss is not acquired, but natural, innate, built-in. Ryle, for once almost "seduced into talking ethics", writes as follows:

> One's knowledge of the difference between right and wrong does not get rusty; we do not keep up our honesty by giving ourselves regular exercises in it. Nor do we excuse a malicious action by saying that we have recently been short of practice in fair-mindedness and generosity. Virtues are not proficiencies. The notion of being out of practice, which is appropriate to skills, is inappropriate to virtues.[1]

Lottin prevents misunderstanding by leaving the Latin word *habitus* throughout his French

[1] In the collection *Essays in Moral Philosophy*, ed. A. I. Melden, Seattle, Washington University, 1958, p. 150.

translation. After all this, I propose to write "habit", hoping to have prevented misunderstanding of Thomist usage by this caveat; there is no suggestion of "habituation". Habits (in scholastic writing) dispose a man to act readily and easily in certain ways, and the particular habit we are to discuss is an inborn power of the mind which enables it readily to grasp and manipulate the basic truths of morality.

(i) THE *COMMENTARY ON THE SENTENCES*

In his *Commentary on the Sentences*,[1] St. Thomas does not set out the questions in Albert's business-like way, but all the points of the old controversy are raised and treated: Synderesis is a habit, the habit of the primary directive principles. His argument is largely *a priori*. We find in nature that all change comes from some dynamic agent, which is itself not changed, and all variety is based on a principle that does not vary; this must hold, too, in operations of the reason. Now, the characteristic activity of reason is to reduce principles to their conclusions, in which process there are many pitfalls. There must, therefore, be some unchanging principle of knowledge which will guarantee the correctness of the reason's operations. When the reason acts in the speculative

[1] *In II Sent.*, dist. 24, q. 2, art. 3.

order, its starting-point is a number of self-evident principles, and the habit by which we possess and recognize these Aquinas calls "intellectus", intelligence, referring to and translating Aristotle's νοῦς.[1] In the same way, when the reason acts in the practical order, it starts from a number of evident principles, and the habit by which we possess and recognize these is called synderesis. It is an acquired habit to the extent that to get it going, to "prime the pump", the terms must be learnt through experience; but it is innate in this sense that, given familiarity with them, the truth of the principles is seen without discursive reasoning.

Thus far St. Thomas' argument. But then comes an unexpected conclusion:

> I therefore conclude, either that synderesis is a habit pure and simple; or at any rate, a faculty supporting a habit which is innate in the sense described.

Nothing in the argument has prepared us for this; apparently Jerome's ghost has not been laid. This impression is confirmed when we see Thomas' restiveness in dealing with the objections. Four times he considers arguments that synderesis is something other than a habit; each

[1] *Nicomachean Ethics*, 1141 a. Ross (Oxford, 1915), translates this, "intuitive reason"; J. A. K. Thomson (Penguin, 1953), "intelligence".

time he rejects them. Yet again in the next article we find him deferring to tradition.

> Synderesis is the name of the habit of the principles, or of a faculty with this habit.

We can see how deep was the influence of Philip's passage quoted above. But in his treatment of questions concerning the properties of synderesis, as distinct from his formal statements on its essential nature, Thomas always speaks of synderesis as a habit, a natural habit by which we readily grasp the basic principles of our moral life.

One such remark is of interest. How is it that in heretics synderesis does not appear to protest against their conduct? St. Thomas makes two suggestions. First, synderesis is essentially natural; it will therefore have nothing to say on questions of faith, which belong to the supernatural order; and it is precisely on matters of faith that a heretic goes astray, while he still may be perfectly sound on matters of natural morality. Second, synderesis is concerned only with goodness at the level of very general principle, e.g. "One must believe whàt God reveals." It is at the level of concrete application that the heretic errs, viz., as to what in fact God has revealed. Hence his first principle is correct, but his conclusion is wrong; it is this that is called his *conscience*.

For on the question of conscience St. Thomas is unambiguous[1]; it is not a faculty nor a habit, but an act. He gives his own version of the "practical syllogism" in which synderesis provides the major, and reason the minor. The judgement of conscience brings them together in a judgement about a concrete, particular act. Hence conscience may be erroneous, even though synderesis is infallible.

(ii) THE *DE VERITATE*

St. Thomas' first teaching period as a Master of Theology in the University of Paris dates from September 1256 to July 1259, and it was during these years that he "disputed" the *Quaestiones Disputatae De Veritate*.[2] One whole question[3] is devoted to the topic of synderesis, taking up in successive articles the three classic questions: Is it a faculty or a habit? Can it err? Can it be extinguished?

[1] *In II Sent.*, dist. 24, q. 3, art. 4.

[2] Aquinas and Bonaventure were appointed to chairs of theology on the same day, 23 Oct. 1256. The University deferred their accession to the degree of doctor and their right officially to occupy their chairs until October 1257. The questions on synderesis and conscience probably date from the last academic year of Thomas' sojourn, 1258–9. Thus Gilson, *History of Christian Philosophy in the Middle Ages*, London, Sheed and Ward, 1955, pp. 685–7, 708–10.

[3] Q. 16.

In dealing with the first of these questions, St. Thomas is plainly unhappy. In his choice and treatment of fifteen objections he seems willing to hold to Jerome's authority by following the compromise of Philip the Chancellor and Albert the Great: Synderesis is "a faculty together with a habit". Yet he puts down five other arguments contending that synderesis is not a faculty, but a habit pure and simple. These he leaves unanswered, as if they really do speak his own mind.

The *corpus articuli* does not help us very much. There is an elaborate *a pari* argument, of the sort dear to the medievals. It is based on the unbroken continuity of created things, and seeks a parallel in the human mind to the intuitive element in the angelic intellect. It leads to the conclusion that synderesis is a habit— "The innate habitual grasp of those first principles of the practical order, which are the first principles of the natural law"—and belongs to the practical reason. Yet still the tradition is too strong, and St. Thomas repeats the conclusion of his *Commentary on the Sentences*:

So, then, the term synderesis either refers exclusively to a natural habit, similar to the habitual possession of the speculative principles; or else it denotes the faculty of reason itself along with this habit.

He seems to show his dissatisfaction with this conclusion by remarking that it does not matter which terminology we adopt.

He is firmer and clearer when he turns from the essential nature of synderesis to its properties, namely, infallibility and incorruptibility. Synderesis cannot err; it provides principles which do not vary, just as the laws that govern the physical universe do not vary. There may be error in applying it in an individual case, either by faulty ratiocination, or by a mistakenly accepted fact. But then it is not synderesis which is wrong, but the judgement of conscience. Thus Christ predicted that the time would come when people who killed the Apostles would consider that they were rendering God a service. But the mistake of such people occurs, not at the level of a universal judgement made by synderesis; at that level they judge rightly that service should be rendered to God. Their mistake occurs at the level of particular fact, believing that the slaying of the Apostles will be pleasing to God.

Can synderesis be extinguished? St. Jerome is recalled in the *Sed contra*: even in Cain's heart synderesis was not extinguished, for he cried, "Guilt like mine is too great to find forgiveness." St. Thomas' answer is a straightforward distinction. In so far as synderesis is a habitual light, it cannot be extinguished any more than can the intellect itself, with its native grasp of the first principles of both the speculative and the practical order. But the action of synderesis may be impeded, both in people who have not attained the use of reason, and in those who have lost this through injury to the bodily organs on which the mind depends in its operation.

The whole of Question Seventeen is devoted to the subject of conscience, and in it St. Thomas has reached what proved to be his final position on the subject. Conscience is neither a faculty nor a habit, but an act. Unfortunately, the linguistic argument he gives, though an acute one, does not hold for the English word "conscience".

He argues that we do not use the same word of a faculty, a habit, and an act, except when the act is proper to that faculty or habit alone. Thus, we can use the word "sight" of the act of seeing, as well as of the faculty, since it applies to seeing alone. But the word "use" may apply to the act of any habit or faculty, and so is not applied to any one alone. Now, says St. Thomas, the word *conscientia* means the application of knowledge to a particular case, and that can take place with any sort of knowledge at all. Therefore, the word "conscience" is to be used only of the act.

However, in modern English, whatever of the

word "science", the word "conscience" is not used of the application of any sort of knowledge to a concrete case, but only of moral knowledge and moral principles. So, on St. Thomas' own linguistic principle, we are entitled to use the word of the moral "sense", and not only of individual moral judgements; indeed, the latter is not the ordinary English usage; we would rather speak of a "judgement of conscience". Still, as we study St. Thomas, we must remember that for him "conscience" designates only the application of general moral principles to a particular case.

The second article argues that an erroneous judgement of conscience may arise in either of two ways, since it is in the conclusion of a practical syllogism. A person may be mistaken in his minor premiss, as are those heretics who believe that all oaths are forbidden by God; or he may reason wrongly, say, by an error in the logical form of his syllogism. On the other hand, a man may form his conscience correctly, but deliberately act against it. This is called acting "with a bad conscience".

(iii) THE *SUMMA THEOLOGICA*

Something like eleven years passed between the writing of the *De Veritate* and the treatment of conscience in the *Summa Theologica*.

It is in the *Pars Prima*[1] that Aquinas deals with the topic of the first chapter of the present book, the terminology and nature of conscience. In the *Prima Secundae* he deals with the power of conscience to oblige, the topic of our second chapter.

It is refreshing to see his firmness and independence in treating the old controversy. Synderesis and conscience are treated in successive articles; St. Jerome's gloss had indeed thus brought them together, but now they are treated together simply because Thomas' theory demands such treatment. He is setting down his own opinions crisply and unambiguously. Jerome's authority is not allowed to influence him at all, though he finds a device to save face for the "spark-of-conscience" tradition.

All the old questions on synderesis are dealt with in one article, "Is synderesis a special faculty, distinct from others?" No, he says, it is not; it is a habit belonging to the reason—to the practical reason,[2] not the will. The proof is the

[1] Q. 79, 12 and 13. Gilson dates this question from the use made (in art. 4) of the Greek-Latin translation of Thomistius' paraphrase of Aristotle's *De Anima*, a translation whose date of publication is known to have been 22 Nov. 1267. (*The Christian Philosophy of St. Thomas Aquinas*, London, Gollancz, 1957, p. 387.)

[2] i.e., the reason when concerned with judging things to be done, as contrasted with the reason when judging things as they are. St. Thomas had explicitly denied that the practical and speculative intellect are separate powers, in the previous article.

old one, but tightly stated. All ratiocination must begin from some principles which are "given", or it would never begin at all. The first self-evident principles for speculative reasoning do not belong to a special faculty, but to an innate habit, the *νοῦς* or intuitive reason of Aristotle. So the first self-evident principles for practical, moral reasoning do not belong to a special faculty, but to a special habit, which is called synderesis. These habits cannot be lost as long as a man enjoys the use of his reason.

St. Thomas recalls the objection, that Jerome seems to put synderesis on a footing with the faculties of reason, irascible appetite and concupiscible appetite. He replies that Jerome's division refers to different acts, not to different faculties. This is fairly obviously not so, but it saves face for St. Jerome; and it shows how finally St. Thomas has shed any feeling for synderesis as a "habit-like faculty".

He is equally decisive in the following article on conscience. Properly speaking, conscience is neither a faculty nor a habit, but an act: the act of applying knowledge to conduct. He supports this first with a rather cavalier etymological argument: "*Conscientia* is formed from *cum alio scientia*"; and the application of knowledge to a particular case is performed by an action.

More seriously, he argues from the normal usages of the word "conscience". It is said to testify; to bind or incite; and to accuse or reproach. These indicate the three ways that we may apply knowledge to conduct.

The first is encountered when we "are conscious of" having done something, and in this sense conscience is said to testify. This seems an unsound point in the article, for it is difficult to see that in this phenomenon there is any application of general principles to the individual case. St. Thomas would probably have been helped by the distinction made in English between "consciousness" and "conscience".

In a second way of applying knowledge to conduct, we make the judgement of conscience that something should be done, or not done. It is in this sense that conscience is said to bind, or incite. Here we have the concept of "legislative conscience" introduced, as we have seen, by St. Paul.

In a third way of applying knowledge to conduct, we make the judgement of conscience that some action already performed was well done, or ill. It is in this sense that conscience is said to excuse, accuse or reproach. This is the usage we have styled "judicial conscience".

St. Thomas holds that these are the proper uses of the word "conscience". They all follow the application of knowledge to conduct, and hence, properly speaking, conscience is an act.

He notes, however, that common usage often

identifies a faculty or a habit with its act, and a cause with its effect. It is thus that he accommodates as common,[1] though less correct, usages the descriptions of conscience we have mentioned through this chapter. St. Basil's "natural power of judgement" is the faculty from which a conscience comes, St. Jerome's synderesis the habit, the Damascene's "law of our mind" the formal cause. An answer to an objection extends this to allow the word "conscience" to be used for synderesis, the habitual grasp of the fundamental moral principles. This resembles more closely modern English usage. St. Bonaventure's definition of conscience comes very close to the contemporary meaning of conscience, which credits it with providing the directions for all our moral life, and applying to all moral judgements, both universal principles and particular applications.

3. Modern Thomists

Modern Thomists follow St. Thomas closely in their formal statements of terminology on this matter. In them conscience is a judgement of the practical reason, drawn from general principles provided by synderesis, on the

[1] It is probably respect for the Fathers that moves him to allow this departure from the principle of common usage given in the *De Veritate*, q. 17, art. 1, discussed above.

morality of an individual action to be done by us. Prümmer's statement is typical:

> *Synderesis* is the habitual grasp of the first moral principles; its function is to dictate *in general* that good should be done and evil avoided ... The function of *conscience* is to decide in a *particular* case what is to be done or avoided. Conscience is capable of error, synderesis is not.[1]

Prümmer shows the continuity of the tradition when he comes to explain the difference between synderesis, natural law, and conscience; he is quite happy to explain how the terms are used today by quoting St. Thomas without qualification:

> Natural law denotes the principles themselves, the universal principles of the law; synderesis, the habitual grasp of them; conscience, an application, after the fashion of a conclusion, of the natural law to something which should be done.[2]

[1] M. Prümmer, *Manuale Theologiae Moralis*, Fribourg, Herder, 1958, vol. 1, pp. 197–8.

[2] *In II Sent.*, dist. 24, q. 2, art. 3, quoted by Prümmer, vol. 1, pp. 197–8.

3. THE PROBLEM OF CONTENT

ST. THOMAS' idiom is unfamiliar to the modern reader, but his problems are at least as fresh as the first chapter of Mill's *Utilitarianism*:

> The intuitive, no less than what may be termed the inductive, school of ethics, insists on the necessity of general laws. They both agree that the morality of an individual action is not a question of direct perception, but of the application of a law to an individual case ... Yet they seldom attempt to make out a list of the *a priori* principles which are to serve as the premises of the science.[1]

This suggests indeed how authentic a part of traditional moral study are the medieval debates outlined above; and it points to the very place where St. Thomas leaves us puzzled. A judgement of conscience, he says, is the conclusion of a practical syllogism whose major is provided by synderesis. Its precision and its validity will therefore be largely determined by the precision with which synderesis can enunciate this major, and the certainty with which we can establish it. It is vexing to find that St. Thomas leaves us rather uncertain about the content of synderesis.

[1] Ch. 1.

It is the habit of the first moral principles; but what are these?

1. "GOOD SHOULD BE DONE"

The obvious candidate is "Good should be done and evil avoided." This is variously described by St. Thomas and his followers as the first principle of the natural law, the supreme principle, the primary principle, the principle on which all others are based, the principle to which all others are reduced.

Now, as it stands in this flat, drab form, such a principle would promise little effect on our moral life. Could it be that synderesis phrases it in some more piquant form, as one person may try to persuade another with such colloquial pleonasms as, "A man's got to do the right thing"? This is not, of course, to translate the first principle into another of different meaning; but perhaps it is the function of synderesis to lend pungency and effectiveness to what would otherwise be without any real sting, without any influence on our moral choices and decisions, as distinct from our moral judgements. We might compare the inscription on the temple at Delos:

Justice is loveliest, and health is best,
And sweetest to obtain is heart's desire.[1]

[1] Thus the *Nicomachean Ethics*, trans. Thomson, p. 42.

That second line can be translated without loss of meaning, "What we like best is what we want most"—as pedestrian a tautology as may be. But its poetic expression strikes chords in us that the prose statement never could.

Is it something like this that synderesis does? That is, lend a more ringing or moving note to the principle, "Good should be done and evil avoided", though making it no less tautologous? This would certainly measure up to the description of synderesis as "inciting us to what is good and drawing us back from evil". In more modern terms, perhaps it is a sense of the difference between right and wrong; not a list of what things are right and wrong, but an acute sense of the general distinction.

However, this is not enough. St. Thomas claims a lot more for synderesis than that it stimulates a relish for good and a distaste for evil; it is to do so in a special way; it provides the major of a practical syllogism.

> Synderesis is said to incite us to what is good and draw us back from what is evil in the sense that from its first principles we proceed to new ones, and pass judgement on these when we reach them.[1]

Now, the principle, "Good should be done and evil avoided", will not serve as the major of

[1] *ST*, 1,79,12c.

a syllogism. It is analytic and necessary, telling us nothing about the facts. Trethowan calls it a "mere tautology, which of itself will lead us no-where",[1] for the whole difficulty would then recur in the minor; how would one prove, "But paying debts is good", "But killing is bad", and so on? For either this minor would need proof, or it would not. If it did not, then it, too, would belong to synderesis. If it did, it would need some other, logically prior, more general major for its own demonstration; and this latter major should belong to synderesis.

We are led, then, to reject the candidature of "Good should be done and evil shunned" as the major of a practical syllogism provided by synderesis. What, then, is its role? It seems to be a purely formal principle, providing the rule that governs all our moral reasoning, rather than its universal premiss. For, though analytic and necessary, it is by no means meaningless. It can be quite meaningfully translated, "It makes no sense to say, 'X is good, but do not desire or pursue X.'" It is therefore in similar logical case in the practical order to the principle of non-contradiction in the speculative; each is a purely formal principle.

It is easy to be deceived by St. Thomas' style

[1] Illtyd Trethowan, "The Philosophical Concept of Morality", in the symposium *The Springs of Morality*, London, Burns Oates, 1956, p. 9.

and method into thinking of him as having a rigidly deductive system. In his metaphysical writings he often speaks of "referring" self-evident propositions to the principle of non-contradiction, or says that they are all "founded" upon it. But it is a mistake to think that he is claiming they are all deduced from it; he is merely saying that to deny these propositions will involve one in contradiction. The principle of non-contradiction is the formal principle that governs all our speculative reasoning.

I think the same is true of the principle "Good should be done and evil avoided" in St. Thomas' ethical system. Of it he uses the same phrases; more particular moral precepts are "founded" on it, or "referred" to it.[1] It is self-evident in the strict sense; if someone says "X is good", it is nonsense to agree that it is, and to ask whether it is something that should be desired or pursued. This is the principle that runs through and controls all our moral reasoning; but it is not the initial premise from which all the rest are deduced. Father Copleston puts this happily:

Aquinas did not think that we can deduce the proposition that to have sexual intercourse with someone else's wife is wrong from the precept that good is to be pursued and evil avoided simply by contemplating, as it were,

[1] *ST*, 1–2,94,2c.

this latter precept. We can no more do this than we can deduce from the principle of non-contradiction the proposition that a thing which is white all over cannot at the same time be red all over.[1]

It is as well to stress this point about the logical status of "Good should be done and evil avoided" as a purely formal principle. Vermeersch, usually so careful, seems to have overlooked it; he writes:

> Thanks to the inborn habit of synderesis, we readily know the most universal moral principles, e.g. *Good should be done and evil shunned; Laws should be obeyed: Promises should be kept.*[2]

Once we have paused to study the logical behaviour of these three propositions, we have no such temptation to identify them. The latter two are moral precepts or rules, well-fitted to act as major premises in moral syllogizing. But the first is, rather, a logical principle which governs such moral syllogizing; the important thing is that we constantly use it, not that we readily enunciate it; it does not matter very much if we never explicitly formulate it at all. So let us

[1] F. C. Copleston, *Aquinas*, Penguin, 1955, p. 223.
[2] A. Vermeersch, *Theologiae Moralis Principia*, Rome, 1923, vol. 1, p. 289.

venture a different suggestion about the content
of synderesis.

2. GENERAL PRINCIPLES OR PRIMARY PRECEPTS?

No doubt it is the self-evidence of the principle
"Good must be done and evil avoided" which
has recommended its candidature as the datum
of synderesis. But to be accurate, St. Thomas
nowhere demands self-evidence for this role.
Synderesis is simply to provide "the first
principles of conduct, built into us by nature",
"the first principles of human conduct". What
sort of principles are these? More likely, perhaps, what he calls the primary precepts of the
natural law, e.g., "Perjury is wrong." This would
do very nicely as the major of a syllogism; the
minor would often be readily provided by contemplating the proposed action, e.g., "To swear
this oath would be perjury." The judgement of
conscience would then be clear: "To swear this
oath would be wrong."

We may make St. Thomas' approach clearer
by thinking of it in reference to modern ethical
controversy. Immediately one is struck by the
resemblance to Mr. Hare. On the point where
he is at odds with Professor Stevenson he is at
one with St. Thomas. Hare and Stevenson are
agreed that moral arguments between people

may always break down, but they differ in their
explanation of this. For Stevenson, if R and E
stand respectively for a set of reasons and an
ethical conclusion, we cannot infer E from R,
whether deductively or inductively[1]; the connection is not logical, but causal; it will be
idiosyncratic to each person, depending on the
individual's psychological attitudes.

> Suppose that a person should tabulate the
> "valid" inferences from R's to E's. It is diffi-
> cult to see how he could be doing anything
> more than specify what R's he thereby resolves
> to accept as supporting the various E's.[2]

So for Stevenson, the connection between the
relevant reasons and the ethical conclusion is
not logical but psychological and causal; moral
arguments are always liable to break down because such connections are personal and idiosyncratic.

Not so for Hare. For him, as for St. Thomas,
one argues to a particular moral judgement by
a syllogistic ratiocination, which must obey the
usual rules for logical validity. There will be a
universal value-judgement for the major premiss,
e.g., "Stealing is wrong." The minor will be
descriptive, e.g., "To take this money would be

[1] C. L. Stevenson, *Ethics and Language*, Yale, 1944,
p. 153.
[2] Stevenson, pp. 170–1.

stealing." So one reaches, by a normal inference-pattern, the judgement of conscience, "To take this money would be wrong."

Where Aquinas and Hare differ, of course, is in the account of that major. For both of them, "Stealing is wrong" will not serve as a "given" initial premiss; some further argument is needed to establish that, and this will require a new major. For St. Thomas, there are a number of general moral principles which, as we shall soon see him hold, are readily grasped by all adults, so that all men begin moral arguments from common premisses. But for Hare, each man is forced back to a number of principles which he simply chooses for himself. Though Hare will maintain, quite consistently, that it is a function of value-judgements to guide choices, none the less one's first value-judgements are a matter of choice. This choice is not the recognition of several principles which are in some way self-evident; it is an individual decision to base one's conduct on these values rather than those, not capriciously made, but in the context of "a complete specification of the way of life of which it is a part". In practice, Hare thinks, such a complete specification cannot be given, the best attempts to do so having been made by the great religions. Still, if one imagines it to have been given, and an inquirer persists in asking "But why *should* I live like that?":

We can only ask him to make up his own mind which way he ought to live; for in the end everything rests upon such a decision of principle.[1]

One is reminded of Hume's famous passage:

It appears evident that the ultimate ends of human action can never, in any case, be accounted for by *reason*, but recommend themselves entirely to the sentiments and affections of mankind, without any dependence on the intellectual faculties.[2]

At the back of many such discussions, of course, there is a logical point. First made in Hume's even more famous "No-Ought-From-Is" passage,[3] it is now so widely accepted that Mr. Prior can write:

The perception that information about our obligations cannot be logically derived from premises in which our obligations are not mentioned has become a commonplace, though perhaps only in philosophical circles.[4]

Hare states the principle forcefully in the framework of his own prescriptive theory—

[1] Hare, p. 69.

[2] *Enquiries*, ed. Selby-Bigge, Oxford, 1902, p. 293.

[3] *Treatise of Human Nature*, Everyman ed., vol. 2, pp. 177–8.

[4] A. N. Prior, *Logic and the Basis of Morals*, Oxford, 1956, p. 36.

> No imperative conclusion can be validly drawn from a set of premisses which does not contain at least one imperative[1]

though he later warns us that one of the premisses may often be "covertly evaluative".[2] Hare and Stevenson are therefore, partly at least, led to their contention by the idea that factual statements cannot, of themselves, logically entail value-judgements; so it is for each man to *decide* which facts he will accept as relevant in framing his value-judgements. The "No-Ought-from-Is" principle has been under heavy attack recently, and its supporters have some serious arguments to answer[3]; but this is not the place to study them.

For St. Thomas, there are a number of general moral principles which, thanks to synderesis, are readily apprehended and accepted by all men, and can serve as the initial premisses in everyone's moral arguments. It is natural to think of Reid's reply to Hume:

> The first principles of morals are not deductions. They are self-evident; and their truth, like that of other axioms, is perceived without

[1] Hare, p. 28.

[2] Hare, p. 92.

[3] e.g., P. R. Foot, "Moral Arguments", in *Mind*, Oct. 1958; "Moral Beliefs", in *Proceedings of the Aristotelian Society*, Dec. 1958; G. E. M. Anscombe, "On Brute Facts", *Analysis*, Jan. 1958.

reasoning or deduction. And moral truths, that are not self-evident, are deduced, not from relations quite different from them, but from the first principles of morals.[1]

This is very much like St. Thomas' model. The principles given by synderesis are rather like axioms from which, theorem-like, moral precepts are deduced with greater or less facility. But here we must be careful. For Aquinas at least, the first moral principles are like the axioms only in their logical primacy—not in the way they are self-evident. They are not analytic propositions, seen to be true simply by studying the meaning of their subject and predicate. In St. Thomas' theory, the clue to the evidence of the ethical "axioms" lies in *natural inclination*.

A full-scale study of his theory would have to work this out thoroughly, showing just what it is that St. Thomas means by "natural inclination": not the psychological impulses of this or that individual, but the ontological tendencies or propensities of human nature in general. Such a study is not the concern of the present book, though the point may become a little clearer when exemplified in the final chapter. Here it is enough to distinguish St. Thomas' view from those ethical theories which Hare calls

[1] "Essays on the Active Powers", 5, 7, in the *Works*, Edinburgh, 1863, vol. 2, p. 675.

"Cartesian", which try to deduce particular duties from some self-evident first principle; a procedure which he thinks (as would St. Thomas) as illusory in morals as it is in science. The Thomist first principles are immediately evident in some sense, since they are to be the premisses from which moral syllogisms begin; but not in the sense that they are analytic. They are evident only in the sense that a person who reflects upon his nature will soon see that certain things are good for him and certain things are bad. St. Thomas does not think, as did Ross and Prichard, that one "intuits" these principles; one sees that "X is good and to be pursued" only if one sees first that X represents the satisfaction of a natural human inclination; all those things towards which human nature has a natural inclination are recognized by the practical reason as good. The propositions that express these are not immediate, therefore, in the sense that the subject is a portmanteau term in the course of whose unpacking the predicate will emerge. They are immediate in the sense that they have no *logical* intermediary, no middle term by means of which the predicate is *inferred* to belong to the subject; this is seen by means of reflecting on one's natural inclinations. I am not sure that this is so very different from Hume:

It is needless to push our researches so far as to ask, why we have humanity or a fellow-feeling with others. It is sufficient, that this is experienced to be a principle in human nature. We must stop somewhere in our examination of causes; and there are, in every science, some general principles, beyond which we cannot hope to find any principle more general. No man is absolutely indifferent to the happiness and misery of others. The first has a natural tendency to give pleasure; the second, pain. This every one may find in himself.[1]

There is a faintly apologetic note about this that is not in St. Thomas' account at this point; but may it not at least be said that for both of them there are moral principles which are logically primary, given, not by analysis of a concept into its components, but by reflection on experience?

At all events, St. Thomas suggests that human nature has such inclinations from three sources: as substance, man has the inclination towards self-preservation; as animal, the inclination to sexual intercourse between man and woman and to the education of children; as rational, the natural inclination to know the truth about God, and towards life in society.[2] Now, if these

[1] *Enquiries*, p. 219, *n*. 1.
[2] *ST*, 1–2,94,2c.

goods and inclinations are to be pursued in an orderly and harmonious way, considerable skill and fairly elaborate reasoning will be called for, and some order of priorities will need to be fixed. The further we descend towards particularity, the more room there will be for disagreement. In this Aquinas was perhaps more acute than Hume. Hume wrote:

> The notion of morals implies some sentiment common to all mankind which recommends the same objects to general approbation and makes every man, or most men, agree in the same opinion or decision concerning it. It also implies some sentiment, so universal and comprehensive as to extend to all mankind, and render the actions and conduct even of persons the most remote, an object of applause and censure, according as they agree or disagree with that rule of right which is established.[1]

This seems to overlook the familiar fact that, at some levels of logical generality, there is indeed widespread agreement, but at others the sharpest of dissent. St. Thomas makes provision for this, as we may illustrate by reference to sexual morality. When he speaks of the natural inclination to sexual intercourse between man and woman, and to the education of children, he is

[1] *Enquiries,* p. 272.

not referring merely to the animal impulse of the erotic urge and the animal instinct of parental affection; he is also claiming that man has a natural inclination to all those actions and restraints implicit in the orderly attainment of the good proper to these drives and instincts. So far, so good; it is when we begin to explicate these actions and restraints that difficulties begin to grow.

First, without any discursive reasoning we can recognize that sexual relationship needs some form of regulation. At that level of generality there is not much trouble; people who are aware that it is through sexual intercourse that children are generated realize that the act of sex is of peculiar moment, dignity and significance; it is in entirely different case from other pleasures which may be capriciously or casually indulged. This is not to say much, but it means that all adults readily arrive at some such conviction as, "Sexual relationship needs some form of regulation", or "Promiscuity is wrong."

Second, a little reflection on experience leads to the conclusion that a woman should have only one husband at a time. For experience shows that a child is properly loved, cared for and educated only when it is known who are his parents; and paternity cannot be known when a woman has several men. When such data of experience are applied, whether formally or implicitly, to our first very general principle, we infer some such conclusion as "Polyandry is wrong." At this level agreement is widespread, but by no means universal.

Third, more detailed study of experience and more elaborate reasoning lead to the conclusion that a man should have only one wife at a time: "Polygamy is wrong." At this level agreement is far from being universal: millions of Mohammedans have disagreed systematically for centuries.

In the light of this account we can understand St. Thomas' terms. The second- and third-level judgements here described he usually calls the primary and secondary precepts of the natural law. They have two possible sources of error: they involve an appeal to one's experience of actual human conduct, and a logical inference when this is applied to the first-level principles. These first-level principles will be, e.g., *not* "Adultery is wrong", nor "Contraception is wrong", *but* "Sexual conduct must be ordered by some rules"; or again, *not* "Killing is wrong" nor "Lynching is wrong", *but* "Killing a man is different from killing a rabbit." Here there is no need for an appeal to experience or for a logical inference; so St. Thomas believed that everyone who has the use of reason is readily capable of mastering and manipulating such principles, "the first principles of human conduct, built into us by nature". As St. Jerome would say, this was the spark that was not quenched even in the heart of Cain. St. Thomas holds that these principles cannot be altered or overridden even by God himself.

So we are now in a position to avoid two opposite extremes in misunderstanding natural-law theory, at any rate as held by Aquinas. One mistake is to present it as explaining morality simply as hearing and obeying the will of God. Thus, Professor Melden writes of some accounts of exceptions to moral laws:

> Such locutions are vestigial relics of an older view, no longer held generally by moral philosophers, of the source of morality—the conception of morality as founded upon the natural law imposed upon his creatures by the will of God. On such a view it does make sense to speak of violations of the law, . . . of exceptions that are or can be made for agents and by agents by God and by Godfrey.[1]

Whatever version of natural-law theory is thus in question, it is certainly not Aquinas'. What has been said will have made it clear that he does not think of morality as something arbitrarily imposed by the will of God; it is discovered by man's reason in reflection on his

[1] A. I. Melden, *Rights and Right Conduct*, Oxford, Blackwell, 1959, p. 43.

natural inclinations, given him by God as creator of human nature, not by God as lawgiver. Things are not wrong because God forbids them; God forbids them because they are wrong. As for the flippancy of God and Godfrey, the notion that natural-law theory means that God can alter or dispense from moral principles at will, one example will show how foreign this is to St. Thomas:

St. Paul says, "God remains true to his word; he cannot disown himself".[1] But if God set aside the order of his justice, he would be disowning himself. And so, God is not able to dispense a man from a right relationship to him, nor from subordination to the order of justice he has declared, not even where it is a case of justice as between man and man.[2]

The contrary misunderstanding is to picture Aquinas' theory as totally deductive. Moral principles are not a number of theorems rigidly deduced from a single axiom; they are the product of rational reflection on our natural inclinations. Of course, Aquinas does not mean that synderesis presents us with a number of cut-and-dried statements which we can chant at will as a schoolboy recites Newton's three laws of motion; rather, it refers to the ability to

[1] 2 Tim. 2.13.
[2] *ST*, 1–2,100,8, ad 2.

recognize or elicit the truth and falsity of general
ethical propositions when confronted with them,
and make sound moral judgements which could
not have been made if those initial principles
were not available in readily manipulable form.
I possess them and I apply them, even though I
may not often explicitly formulate them. It is
rather like Ryle's account of how the intellectual
operations "govern" the exercises of other mental
capacities:

> To describe someone as doing something
> which he could not have done without
> formerly having had a certain education does
> not entail saying that he must have recited
> all or any of those early lessons just before he
> acted. I could not now read a Greek sentence,
> if I had not formerly learned Greek grammar,
> but I do not ordinarily have to remind myself
> of any rules of Greek grammar, before I con-
> strue a Greek sentence. I construe according
> to those rules, but I do not think of them. I
> bear them in mind, but I do not appeal to
> them, unless I get into difficulties.[1]

This seems to hit it off very well. It reminds us
that synderesis is a habit, and that we were
tempted to translate St. Thomas' *habitus* as
skill. As we grow in moral maturity we become

[1] *The Concept of Mind*, London, Hutchinson, 1949,
p. 315.

increasingly skilful in choosing and applying the principle relevant to the case in hand without any explicit formulation of first principles at all.

The complaint stands that St. Thomas' terminology is not consistent. In one place[1] he distinguishes between the common and the proper precepts of the natural law thus: The proper precepts are, as it were, conclusions from the common precepts, which themselves are the same for all men. But in the next article he gives the same account of the distinction between primary and secondary precepts. Yet in the next question[2] he presents the distinction between natural law and *jus gentium* in identical terms. In another place[3] this latter distinction is explained as Ulpian had explained it: natural law is that which governs all animals, both rational and irrational; *jus gentium* refers only to that which governs man.

This is certainly a pity. The inconsistencies seem to be due to St. Thomas' anxiety to respect the different terms used by the various Fathers. It certainly muddles our first reading of his treatise on law. But the distinction I have suggested seems authentic enough: there are a number of universal principles, or starting-points, or initial premisses, which are neither the principle "Good must be done and evil

[1] *ST*, 1–2,94,4c. [2] *ST*, 1–2,95,4c. [3] *ST*, 2–2,57,3c.

avoided", nor the primary precepts. They are distinct from the former, because it is not a premiss but a formal principle. They are distinct from the primary precepts, which are not self-evident but themselves the conclusions of ratiocination, and the product of experience and observation.

One last point about synderesis is worth making. In a passage that deserves more attention, St. Thomas remarks that the moral virtues do not dictate the great ends of human conduct; these are given and made known by natural reason, by synderesis. Synderesis points out the ends, and the moral virtues tend towards these ends, being helped in this by *prudentia*, practical wisdom, which prepares the way for them by disposing the means. It is in this sense that practical wisdom sets the other virtues in motion; whereas practical wisdom itself is set in motion by synderesis, as is science by intuitive reason.[1]

Like the rest of St. Thomas' account, this is clear enough, and quite coherent; but it is still not filled in. Human life must not be treated as animal life, sex is important and must be used with the order and thought proper to precious things, reason must play a great part in human living—so far, so good. But what of "We should live temperately and act justly"; "Act only on that maxim whereby thou canst at the same time

[1] *ST*, 2–2,47,6, ad 3.

will that it should become a universal law"; "Do unto others as you would have them do to you" —do these refer to ends or means? Are they principle or precept? Until Aquinas tells us this, his account of synderesis is incomplete, and so also, consequently, is his account of conscience. We cannot yet be quite sure which are the principles all men share, and so we cannot be quite sure what are the limits to which judgements of conscience may extend in all good faith.

But for the purpose of this essay, this defect is not fatal. We shall be concerned with only one aspect of the right to freedom of conscience, namely, matters of religious choice, profession and practice. We can quite well follow and appraise St. Thomas' views on this provided we have his general description of how conscience works; and on this he is clear enough.

For this chapter has simply set out what St. Thomas holds to be the nature and working-method of conscience: what it is and how it works at the purely descriptive level. Now we turn to the evaluative level, to the ability of conscience to create a moral obligation for the human will. This time at least, with clear conscience, we pass from *is* to *ought*.

PART II

PART II

THE BASIS OF THE ARGUMENT: THE AUTHORITY OF CONSCIENCE

B UTLER'S phrase, "the authority of conscience", summarizes very neatly the basis of our argument for freedom of conscience, for we may anticipate that that argument will run somewhat as follows:

I have an absolute moral duty not to act against my conscience, and hence this is a necessary condition of my achieving the end and destiny assigned my human nature. Now the State, civil authority, exists to help me achieve my end, and the powers it has are given it for that purpose. If, therefore, the State forces me to act against my conscience, it is acting beyond its powers and against my rights.

The first major point to make good, then, is the sovereign authority of conscience. This chapter sets out to show first, that St. Thomas established the absolute obligation of never acting against one's conscience (a negative point); second, that he provided the principles for establishing the obligation of always following a judgement of

conscience made in good faith (the positive
corollary).

1. THE DEBATE BEFORE ST. THOMAS

We have seen that the formal scholastic
treatise on conscience began around the year
1230, and traced the main points made about
its nature and function, and the many confusions that prevailed. When we turn to the
authority of conscience as a moral norm, there
is mercifully less tangle. We shall distinguish
three distinct schools of thought before we study
St. Thomas' writings, and we shall find that, by
espousing the cause of conscience, he broke with
the common opinion of his immediate pre-
decessors.

There was no "authority" here of such
dominant influence as the paragraph from St.
Jerome's Commentary on Ezechiel. Two texts,
however, frequently recurred and set the limits
between which the debate moved. On one side
there was a celebrated comment on St. Paul's
principle, "All that is not of faith is sin."[1] The
Glossa Interlinearis, an influential Scripture
commentary written by Anselm of Laon, remarked that "faith" in this verse does not mean
the theological virtue by which we believe on

[1] Rom. 14.23, Douay Version. The Knox version
makes the point clear without benefit of gloss:
"Wherever there is bad conscience, there is sin."

the authority of God, but conscience. It comments:

> *All*, even though intrinsically good, *that is not of faith*, i.e., that is so against conscience that we believe it to be evil, *is sin*.

On the other side stood a remark of St. Augustine, which many medieval moralists invoked as the basis for an argument against the authority of conscience:

> The command of a subordinate authority does not bind if it runs counter to the command of a superior in authority; as for instance, if the proconsul were to enjoin what the Emperor forbade.[1]

The argument from this looked a good one. Conscience has no authority except that which it receives as God's delegate; if, therefore, conscience commands something against God's law, we are bound not to follow it; just as, if the proconsul commands something against the Emperor's law, we are bound not to obey him.

Once again, the thirteenth-century writings on the question have been assembled by Lottin.[2] He has arranged them according to the religious obedience of the authors: first Franciscans,

[1] *Sermo VI De Verbis Domini*, cap. 8.
[2] *Psychologie et morale aux 12ᵉ et 13ᵉ siècles*, Louvain, 1948, vol. 2, pp. 354–406.

second secular masters, third Dominicans. But
we are interested in the controversy only in so
far as it gives the antecedents of St. Thomas'
position; so let us rather arrange them into the
three categories into which opinion fell.

1. CONSCIENCE NEVER BINDS

St. Augustine's parallel with proconsul and
Emperor seemed to argue that nothing done
against God's law can be exempt from the guilt
of sin. On the other hand, St. Paul and his
commentators clearly demanded that some
deference be shown to the dignity of conscience.
The first attempt at resolving this dilemma was
made by Alexander of Hales.

Alexander, writing about the year 1230,[1] adverts to the contemporary scholastic analysis of
a human act. In judging its morality one must
consider the object of the act and the circumstances of its performance; the latter includes
the personal intention of the agent.

Some acts have an object which is essentially
good, such as loving God; no circumstances can
make them evil. Some acts have an object which
is essentially bad, such as fornication; no circumstances can make them good. Should conscience
be mistaken in these cases there is no obligation

[1] *Commentary on the Sentences*, in dist. 39, art. 2.
Quoted by Lottin, pp. 354-7.

to follow it, and indeed to follow it would be sinful. For any power that conscience might have comes from God; he quotes St. Paul, "Authority comes from God only, and all authorities that hold sway are of his ordinance",[1] so any suggestion that it makes against God's law is made *ultra vires*. It is absolutely necessary to put away the error.

This is our first meeting with the baffling phrase, "One's duty is to put away the error", which is to bedevil all the scholastic discussions on the authority of conscience. Surely the really vexed case is the one where the error is unconscious, where a man genuinely believes his judgement is correct and has no suspicion that his opinion runs against the moral law? How is he to "put off" an error of which he is unaware? We shall see St. Thomas consider this problem in his last writing on the subject.

Alexander then takes up the other case. Some acts have an indifferent object, such as eating bread; what if conscience mistakenly judges them to be obligatory or forbidden? Even then, he says, conscience induces no obligation; that could arise only from the command of a superior.

The Secular master Walter of Château-Thierry modified this view verbally, but not in substance. He held that conscience does not bind of itself. but only consequentially. He

[1] Rom. 13.1.

wrote a question on the subject while he was
Chancellor of the Archdiocese of Paris,[1] and it
is to his credit that he first addressed himself
formally to the question that is logically prior,
"Does conscience as such, in general, bind?"
Only then, and in the light of his answer to that
question, does he take up the problem of the
erroneous conscience.

On the question concerning conscience as
such, he gives an interesting picture of the state
of the question in the mid-century. There are
some, he says, who hold that conscience does
impose an obligation, basing their case on the
passage quoted from St. Paul. There are others
who hold that it does not oblige in matters that
are intrinsically good or evil, but does oblige in
matters objectively indifferent. The common
opinion, however, is that conscience does not
bind, but merely teaches and encourages "by
way of suggestion or guidance or stimulus".
Walter accepts this as his own view, and argues
that it is only the legislator who exercises
efficient causality in the matter of creating obligation; the law is merely a quasi-formal cause,
and conscience is even less: it has no causality,
but is only a necessary condition of the law's
reaching the subject. It is in this way that he

[1] Therefore between the years 1246 and 1249. Lottin
discovered the question in Toulouse in 1938, and re-
produces it in full, pp. 379–85.

interprets the remark of Pope Innocent III that whoever acts against conscience "paves the way to hell"; namely, he reveals contempt of the law-giver whose command conscience simply reports.

Walter is thus prepared to answer the question, "Is an *erroneous* conscience binding?" No, he says, it is not; neither in so far as it is erroneous, nor in so far as it is a conscience. In so far as it is erroneous, there is no obligation to follow it; rather, the obligation is to correct it. In so far as it is a conscience, there is no obligation to follow it, for conscience *as* conscience induces no obligation; it creates obligation only in so far as it proclaims the command of the superior, which in this case is precisely what it fails to do. St. Augustine's remark about the Emperor and the proconsul is quoted again to support the argument. For the person with a perplexed conscience, there is no real difficulty: "The error must be put away."

2. CONSCIENCE SOMETIMES BINDS

John de la Rochelle also begins with the logically prior question of the authority of conscience in general. He, too, takes up the text attributed to Pope Innocent III, "Whoever acts against conscience paves the way to hell." John supports the text with an argument that does attempt to offer some proof of the authority of conscience:

Conscience is the sight of what should be done; but to see what should be done, and not do it, is to be in contempt; therefore it is sinful to act against conscience.

He writes at greater length on the problem of the misguided conscience, and this leads him to introduce finer distinctions in evaluating the morality of acts according to their object.

Some objects specify acts as necessarily and essentially good, as loving God above all for his own sake; some objects specify acts as necessarily and essentially evil, as fornication or lying. In these cases, says John, an erroneous conscience induces no obligation, and to follow it is sinful.

But there are some objects which specify acts as good in general, though not always; they may be vitiated by an unworthy purpose—for example, when one gives alms for vainglory. Other acts, evil in general, may become good when prompted by a worthy purpose, as visiting a brothel to save a life. Finally, there are acts whose morality is objectively indifferent, as sifting wheat from straw. In these three cases, conscience, even a misguided conscience, has the force of inducing obligation. For, seeing that there is no law, natural or written, which enjoins or forbids these actions universally, conscience takes the place of law:

In matters that are morally neutral, conscience is my law; for it makes the judgement that a given act should be done because it is the law of God.

We may be inclined to say that John's instinct is better than his argument. For one thing, judicial power is not legislative power; yet the reason given for following conscience in the last three cases is the *judgement* that conscience makes. On the other hand, if such judicial power does happen to be also invested with legislative power, why is this not so in the two earlier cases? Surely I am more probably obliged to do what *I* judge to be God's command than to do what someone else judges it to be? None the less, we can see that Rochelle has helped the argument on its way.

The greatest of the Franciscan doctors, St. Bonaventure, followed the general opinion. A given act is either enjoined by God's law, or untouched by it. We cannot be excused if we break God's law by omitting an act it prescribes, or by performing an act it forbids, on the grounds that we are following conscience:

If a man does what his conscience dictates, and this is against God's law; and if it is a mortal sin to act against God's law: then there can be no doubt that he sins mortally.

The argument of Augustine is invoked: If the Emperor orders one thing and his subordinate, the proconsul, the opposite, it is the Emperor's command we are bound to obey; and conscience holds authority essentially in subordination to God. Nor can we claim that it is a case of "perplexed conscience", or moral dilemma; before we perform the action in question, we must put away the error, so that conscience may be in harmony with God's law. For conscience creates obligation in us, he argues, only when its dictates are in conformity with the will of God or not opposed to the law of God; and this is still true when it is in error. But it cannot sanction acts that are opposed to the will of God. It is in this sense that he interprets the passage quoted above from the *Glossa* on Rom. 14.23. It says that any action done against conscience is sinful, but this refers only to the case where conscience is in harmony with the moral law. In such a case, says Bonaventure, the error must be removed or there is no avoiding sin. Once again we are left feeling that the whole point of the argument has been missed.

3. CONSCIENCE ALWAYS BINDS

St. Albert the Great made one important original contribution, and one valuable amplification. The innovation was his seeing that any account of conscience must study the subjective factor. The amplification was the first attempt to give some meaning to the phrase, "The error should be put away."

In his *Summa de Homine*[1] (*c.* 1230) he takes up the question, "Is conscience always binding?" As we have seen, all previous discussions asked whether conscience, *objectively* true or false, obliges. Albert sees that any question of conscience turns attention to *subjective* states as well as objective matters; he breaks very new ground by claiming that the answer to the question is to be given, not in terms of true or false, but in terms of the subjective firmness with which the judgement of conscience is held. He had earlier analysed this type of "assurance" into five degrees: doubt, ambivalence, opinion, belief, certainty. In terms of this analysis he now answers the question: Where there is merely doubt or ambivalence, conscience creates no obligation; but where there is opinion, belief, or certainty, conscience is binding, whether it be correct or erroneous. No proof is given, but the sovereign authority of conscience has been claimed for the first time in the debate.

Albert's other merit lies in his making the first attempt to explain the phrase, "The error must be put away." He writes:

[1] *Summa de Creaturis*, pt. 2, *Summa de Homine*, q. 72, art. 2.

How is one to put off an erroneous conscience? I reply, by examining the minor premiss assumed by reason. Quite often this is false, and when examined its falsity becomes evident. Thus the conscience ceases to be erroneous.

This is certainly an attempt to make sense of a phrase that had been repeated constantly, but given little meaning. But we can hardly accept it as a successful attempt. First, there is the problem raised at the end of our first chapter— what does the major of the syllogism contain? If it is restricted to matters on which all men are agreed, it will be so vague that it will not provide a middle term in common with the minor. If it is narrowed sufficiently to provide this, it will no longer comprise truths immediately evident to all men. Second, Albert fails to meet the practical problem, Why should a man begin such an examination of his syllogism? How is he to know that he is in error? Still, we see that Aquinas' master was exercised on the point, and not merely repeating what had been commonly held.

2. ST. THOMAS

NO doubt St. Thomas owed a great deal to his master Albert for having broken with the general opinion on the authority of conscience. But what Albert had merely stated, St. Thomas set out to prove. He put forward three new lines of argument for the sovereign authority of conscience, and effectively disposed of Augustine's parallel of the Emperor and proconsul.

1. THE *COMMENTARY ON THE SENTENCES*

In the *Commentary on the Sentences*, St. Thomas considers only the particular question of the misguided conscience: "Does an erroneous conscience bind?"[1] But his conclusion is expressed in general terms: every conscience, true or false, is binding, in the sense that to act against conscience is always wrong.

This is virtually the position taken by Albert, but St. Thomas gives argument for what Albert merely stated. He puts forward a valuable principle: We judge the will by the standard of its own proper object. Now, *the proper object of the will is the good, not as it is in itself, but*

[1] *In II Sent.*, dist. 39, q. 3, art. 3.

as it is presented by the reason; and this is just what we mean by the judgement of conscience. Hence, that which conscience judges (whether correctly or not) to be obligatory, by that very judgement binds the will. On the other hand, if a proposed act is objectively good, but is presented by the reason as evil, the will cannot pursue it without becoming evil. Aquinas does little to strengthen his case by referring to the derivation of the moral verb *obligare* from the physical *ligare* and pointing a parallel: just as a man in physical bonds loses the physical freedom of movement, so a man held by the bonds of conscience loses moral freedom of action. But the crux of the argument is not the verbal parallel, but the sound point that the will is to be judged by the standard of the-good-as-seen. The conclusion is clear: any act done against conscience is morally evil.

It may be as well to pause here for a point of clarification. We shall be frequently meeting the distinction between "the good as it is in itself" and "the good as it is apprehended by the reason"; only the latter, says St. Thomas, is the proper object of the will. This might create an impression of his advocating a sort of idealist dualism, as if we never know the-thing-in-itself, but only our idea of it. That would be a misreading of the distinction. He held the principle, "There is nothing in the intellect which was not

first in the senses"; but he did not think that the
intellect *infers* the external object from sense-
data; we know the external object, he believed,
without any *logical* medium. In the present
argument he is simply stressing the point that
the reason is liable to be mistaken; that what it
judges to be good may not be good in reality;
but that, mistaken or not, it is that judgement
of the reason in whose light the will must be
judged, for it is the good as seen by that judgement which is the proper object of the will.
This is almost identical with something Miss
Anscombe has written:

> We must always remember that an object is
> not what what is aimed at *is*; the description
> *under which* it is aimed at is that under which
> it is *called* the object.[1]

St. Thomas applies the point to the moral
appraisal of an action, concluding that the standard by which we are to judge the performance
of a person's will is the good as he sees the good;
a principle very like the modern colloquialism
that "You must judge a man according to his
lights." St. Thomas accordingly reaches the conclusion that any act done against one's conscience
is bad.

He seems less happy when he turns to the

[1] G. E. M. Anscombe, *Intention*, Oxford, Blackwell,
1958, p. 65.

correlative question, "May we then say that any act done according to conscience is good?" No, he replies; for an act to be morally good it is not enough that I apprehend it as good; it must also *be* good objectively; both subjective and objective elements must be good. But for an act to be morally bad, it is enough that either element be lacking. He quotes the old saying of the Pseudo-Dionysius, "Perfection comes only from a total cause; let one point be missing and the whole is bad." In matters of moral or aesthetic appraisal, it is not enough that there be *some* good features present for an action or a work of art to be pronounced good without qualification; all must be present. The elements of a morally good act include both the object of the act and the intention of the agent. Each is a necessary, but not a sufficient, condition for an act to be evaluated as good *sans plus*. St. Thomas concludes, "The man who follows an erroneous conscience is not exempt from sin."

Now here, one feels, St. Thomas seems to be deserting his own principle. Morality is to be evaluated, he says, by the standard of the will's own proper object. This should mean, not only that if it rejects its own proper object it acts badly, but also that if it embraces its own proper object it acts well. Again, he holds that the only proper object of the will is the good, as the will is shown the good: "The good, not as it is in itself, but as it is presented by the reason." It seems inconsistent, then, to refuse the appraisal "good" to an act on the grounds that the will has failed to pursue something which is not, after all, its own proper object. In other words, St. Thomas seems to be saying that you must follow your conscience only when what your conscience judges to be good is in fact good. But how can conscience possibly *judge* whether its *judgement* corresponds to what is objectively good?

The other unsatisfactory point in the *Commentary on the Sentences* is his treatment of the case of the perplexed conscience. He faces the objection that his reply seems to place a man in a moral dilemma. If he fails to follow an erroneous conscience he sins. If he follows it, he sins. "This implies that, as long as conscience remains in error, a man cannot avoid sin." In such a case a man must inevitably sin; which is surely unreasonable.

After the acute principle which opened the article, his reply seems naïve: a man needs only to put aside his error, and the dilemma is ended. The logic of this seems to be that every error is both conscious and deliberate. Such an assumption seems very odd at a time when there was such lively disagreement among moralists on a great number of problems. Lottin devotes a whole long chapter to the thirteenth-century debates on some of these issues, from Langton up to the end of the century.[1] In each of these debates some moralists were in error, and were just not able to "put the error aside"—nor even agree as to where error lay.

One would have expected a more satisfactory conclusion since, a little earlier in the very same book, St. Thomas had remarked that some ignorance is beyond a man's control, and hence excuses him from any fault:

> Where there is such ignorance that a man is in no way to blame for the ignorance itself, he is wholly free from blame.[2]

But he does not see the bearing of what is conceded here on the problem of erroneous conscience.

This is the more disappointing from the point of view of our whole enquiry concerning freedom of religion, for there is a remark in that same question on ignorance which we should dearly like to see expanded. He writes:

> In any person at all, ignorance is always culpable if it concerns sound morals or the truth of the Faith.[3]

These are dark words.

[1] Pt. 5, ch. 2.
[2] *In II Sent.*, dist. 22, q. 2, art. 2.
[3] *In II Sent.*, dist. 22, Q. 2, art. 1.

First, one would want to ask, what is the meaning here of "sound morals"? The problems which bothered us in the first part of this essay recur at once—the whole difficulty about the primary and secondary precepts. St. Thomas himself believes that mistakes are possible over many derived precepts of the moral law which are not immediately evident to all men. He even takes Julius Caesar's word for it that the Germans did not know the precept, "Stealing is wrong."[1] But it would seem peculiar to say that such precepts did not belong to "sound morals."

Second, what can he mean by saying that ignorance is always culpable when it concerns the truth of the Faith? He must mean such a statement to apply only to Christians who have embraced and professed the Faith, for he admits elsewhere that there is no sin in the disbelief of those to whom the Gospel has never been preached.[2]

Third, we should want to ask whether the statement is intended as a loose generalization (in the sense of, "In most cases such ignorance is blameworthy") or as strictly universal (in the sense of, "Such ignorance can never be without blame"). If it is meant only in the former sense, it is of little interest, and indeed of little service

[1] *ST*, 1–2,94,4c; written, of course, some twelve to fifteen years later.
[2] *ST*, 2–2,10,1c.

to the point he is debating. If it is meant in the latter sense, proof of a very thorough kind would be required to support so serious a claim. But he seems to be making a much larger claim, namely, that a person who has never received the Faith is guilty of culpable ignorance in that regard. We may go further than pointing out that St. Thomas offers no proof of this important claim; we may speculate how one could possibly be produced. The difficulties of establishing it by empirical observation would daunt the most venturesome demographer. On the other hand, an *a priori* proof would always have to contain one premiss which could not be established *a priori*, namely, that the religious truth had been so proposed that it produced a conviction of authenticity, and was then rejected in bad faith.

However, it would be a pity if we were to be so oppressed by these two or three dissatisfactions as to overlook the striking points in the treatment of erroneous conscience in the *Commentary on the Sentences*. A new principle has been brought forward: the will is to be judged by the standard of the good as subjectively apprehended, not as it is objectively in itself. The essence of moral rightness consists in a certain sort of reaction or orientation, or even "posture", of the will—a pro-attitude to the good as apprehended.

2. THE *DE VERITATE*

In the *De Veritate*, St. Thomas devotes the whole of Question Seventeen to the topic of conscience. In this work he does study the relationship of his theory concerning the effect of ignorance on moral responsibility to his theory of erroneous conscience. First, however, he takes up the logically prior question of the authority of conscience as such—"Does conscience bind?" —and establishes a principle which has far-reaching consequences:

> No-one is bound by a law save by one means alone: knowledge of that law.

He comes to this by way of an elaborate parallel between moral and physical "binding", *ligatio*. Binding a body physically puts it under unconditional necessity; it simply cannot move. Binding a will morally puts it under conditional necessity; if it moves in a certain way it will lose its chance of reward. But in each case the necessity is induced by some outside agent. In the case of the will, the agent is the competent authority: "The action by which the will is moved is the command of the ruler and governor." Hence the ruler's command plays the part in binding the will morally which the action of the agent plays in binding a thing physically; and in each case the binding is possible only if the two entities are in contact. In moral matters, contact of subject and ruler is achieved by knowledge. Therefore, no-one is bound by a law save by one means alone: knowledge of that law.

Then how does conscience bind? What is the source of its authority? The parallel with physical binding is pursued. The physical agent produces its effect through contact, and the effect produced by this contact is precisely the same as the effect produced by the agent, for the contact produces its effect only by force of the agent and the agent produces its effect only by means of the contact. It is the same in moral matters, that is, the conditional necessity imposed on the will. "Contact" is made between the will and the precept by means of knowledge. The effect produced by this knowledge is precisely the same as the effect produced by the precept, for the knowledge induces obligation only by force of the precept, and the precept induces obligation only by means of the subject's knowledge of it:

> The command does not bind save by force of knowledge of it, and the knowledge only by force of the command.

But conscience is precisely the application of knowledge of the command to a given act. Therefore conscience is said to create obligation by force of the divine command. (The adjective "divine" is puzzling, since no such qualification has so far been mentioned.)

Here, then, is another new argument. All necessity demands some extrinsic cause, and the cause must be in immediate contact with the thing necessitated. In things of the mind in general, contact is made by knowledge; in questions of obligation specifically, this knowledge is called conscience.

At first sight, it seems a pity that such an important principle should be based on so shaky an argument. "Action at a distance is repugnant" will not be accepted without demur in physical matters. Even if it were, how is one to prove that the parallel, barely stated by St. Thomas, holds in matters of mind and spirit? But at second sight our fears are allayed. We may look on the remarks about physical contact as mere illustration; the principle would seem to stand on its own feet. Let us shed the parallel, and we still have a valid argument:

> A subject is not bound by the command of a king or prince unless the command reaches him. But it reaches him through knowledge. Hence no-one is bound by a law save by one means alone: knowledge of that law.

This seems to be a basic principle for our whole project. We may support our claim, that it holds good without the appeal to the parallel with physical contact, by referring to an early attack on the article. The Franciscan, Walter of Bruges, writing[1] in the year 1267, about ten years after the *De Veritate*, supported his master Bonaventure quoted above, and attacked the argumentation of St. Thomas. Action at a distance may be impossible in the physical world, he says; but there is nothing to prove it impossible among spiritual entities. It is therefore not proven that the same power is at work in the divine precept and in conscience. Indeed, it is not true; it is the divine precept which is the true *cause* of obligation in man; conscience is only its necessary *condition*, he claims. But against him, we may reply that this is all that is necessary to uphold St. Thomas' principle. Even if conscience were only a necessary condition of obligation, it would still follow that without knowledge of a precept there is no obligation in its regard.

St. Thomas derives two corollaries from this. First, a person who is incapable of knowing a precept is not bound by it. Second, a person who does not know it is not bound by it, "except in so far as he is obliged to know it". This last proviso is puzzling, but it will be better discussed a little further on.

[1] *Quaestiones disputatae*, q. 12, quoted by Lottin, pp. 399–403.

The answer to one of the objections is note-worthy (ad 4um). The objection is this: The authority which can bind can also set free; but conscience cannot absolve a man; so it cannot bind him either. Aquinas answers with a distinction. An erroneous conscience does not excuse a person, when he sins by the very error itself, as happens when he errs about things he is obliged to know. But it does excuse him if the error concerns matters he is not under an obligation to know, as happens when he is ignorant about a matter of fact.

There are two things to notice here. First, St. Thomas holds that ignorance of fact can be an excusing ignorance. He has held elsewhere that ignorance of law cannot. Second, we meet again the difficult phrase, "If he is mistaken about things which he has an obligation to know." What if a man does not know that he is bound to know them? Here, surely, Thomas' own principle tells against him; there can be no obligation about his duty to know "save by one means only: knowledge of that duty". In other words, we are agreeing with the principle, but suggesting that he has not carried its application right through; right through, that is, to the case, "Knowledge of the law which commands him to know it." On his own principle, it is not enough to show that I am bound to know a certain law; it must also be shown that I *know* I am bound to know it.

ERRONEOUS CONSCIENCE

Article Four is then devoted to the question of erroneous conscience. If conscience holds authority only in so far as it expresses the will of God, how can an erroneous conscience be binding, since it does not express God's will?

St. Thomas begins by quoting the view that an erroneous conscience does not bind in things that are intrinsically evil, but does bind in matters objectively indifferent. In rebuttal of this view, he asks, "What is it to say that conscience binds?" He replies that it is to say, "If a man acts against his conscience he sins"; it is not to say, "If he follows conscience, he acts well." The reason is that, if this were so, the (evangelical) counsels would be obligatory. But this is precisely the difference between the counsels and the precepts, that it is no sin to neglect the former. The phrase "conscience obliges" does not mean that following it is good, but that acting against it is evil.

He then states his own position: If conscience, rightly or wrongly, declares an action to be commanded by God, and a man decides to do the opposite, he cannot avoid sin. The reason he gives is simple, and it seems to be decisive: "As

far as lies within him, a man is determined not
to obey the will of God." There seems to be no
answer to this, given his careful definition of
terms; and he hastens to stress the limits of his
position: seeing that it is an erroneous conscience, the error should be removed, and the
judgement of conscience reversed; but while it
stands it is binding.

The second objection is the familiar one from
St. Augustine: The precept of a lower power,
such as a proconsul, does not bind against a
contrary ordinance from his superior, such as
the Emperor; but an erroneous conscience is inferior to God, and runs counter to his ordinance;
hence it cannot be binding. St. Thomas disposes
of this firmly and briefly. Such a principle holds
only when the superior and the inferior each
issue a command, and each command, separately
and distinctly, is presented to the subject; then
the higher authority obliges. But this is not the
case here; conscience is precisely the presenta-
tion of the divine command to the subject. The
true parallel, says St. Thomas, would obtain if
the only way that the Emperor's precept ever
reached the subject were by way of the proconsul. In that case, despising the proconsul
would be on a par with despising the Emperor,
whether the proconsul relayed his superior's
wishes truthfully or not.

The answer to the fifth objection makes ex-

plicit a principle previously implied. Because
of the distinction made in the answer, let us
quote it verbatim:

> God is more merciful than any earthly ruler.
> But an earthly ruler does not hold a person
> guilty of an offence for something done in
> error. Much less, then, will God hold a man
> guilty of sin for following an erroneous
> conscience.

He replies:

> The conclusion is correct when the error itself
> is sinless, as when it arises from ignorance of
> fact. But if it arises from ignorance of law, the
> conclusion is not correct, because then the
> ignorance is itself a sin.

He is claiming, then, that ignorance of a matter
of fact excuses, and ignorance of the law does
not. This seems very odd.

On the one hand, there can often be matters
of fact about which ignorance is blameworthy.
We may think of a doctor who operates without
knowing whether his instruments are sterilized,
an aircraft navigator who has not assured himself of the accuracy of his instruments, a signal-
man who does not inform himself of changes in
the time-table of trains. One could quickly draw
up a frightening litany of cases of culpable
ignorance in matters of fact.

On the other hand, it is surprising to find St. Thomas saying so flatly that ignorance of the law is always blameworthy. First, of which law is he speaking? If it is the natural moral law, the old difficulty recurs of arriving at a satisfactory list of the principles given by synderesis, and the notorious diversity of opinion as moral rules become more specific and applied. If it is divine positive law, we have already noticed that St. Thomas himself was to hold that unbelief is no sin in lands where the Gospel has not been preached. "How shall they believe in him of whom they have not heard?" Second, no proof whatever is offered for this very important claim. Aquinas makes reference to a "secular judge", who will not accept ignorance of the law as an excuse. But the procedural rules of a court for the external forum prove nothing about the interior, personal guilt or innocence of one who is not aware of his obligations. Third, the assertion that ignorance of the law does not excuse from its obligation seems to be in direct contradiction to St. Thomas' own principle, "No-one is bound by a law save by one means alone: knowledge of that law." This principle he *has* proved, and it would seem to rule out the later unsupported assertion.

The eighth objection calls for another attempt to solve the problem of the moral dilemma. On the one hand, it is always sinful to act against

one's conscience; yet apparently there are cases
when it is sinful to follow it. In such cases it
would seem that a man will be sinning, whatever he does. St. Thomas merely gives the
answer[1] that most writers have given before him:
The error has to be removed, the faulty judgement put right; this is the only way—but he
thinks that it *is* a way—of avoiding sin. At this
stage let us merely protest that this answer is
not good enough, given the weakness we have
just found in his account of ignorance.

3. THE *DE MALO*

Before taking St. Thomas' final treatment of
the question, it is interesting to see that the
black-and-white attitude concerning ignorance
of fact and ignorance of law adopted in the
De Veritate was somewhat mitigated in the
more mature *De Malo*.[2]

It makes the distinction between two categories of ignorance, ignorance of law and
ignorance of fact, and refers them to Aristotle's
distinction between universal ignorance and
particular ignorance. It points out that there
can be blameless ignorance of the law, even of

[1] Ad 8 um. There seems to be a slip in his reply, in
that it refers to error concerning the sinfulness of
fornication, which the objection had not mentioned.

[2] Q. 2, art. 2. The *De Malo* probably dates from the
Paris sojourn of 1267–9.

the moral and divine law; and on the other hand, ignorance of matters of fact can be culpable if it occurs in circumstances where there is a duty to enquire.

This is applied to the question of the culpability of the ensuing act. Voluntary and culpable ignorance never excuses from sin, whether it concerns matters of fact or of law. On the other hand, involuntary and blameless ignorance always excuses, whichever it concerns. A man who, after taking reasonable care, believes that his target is a stag and kills his father, is innocent of parricide; but a man who means to kill his father and kills a stag in mistake for his father, incurs the moral guilt of parricide.

4. The *Summa Theologica*

We are thus prepared to see the absolute position of the earlier writings modified in St. Thomas' most mature work, the *Summa Theologica*.[1] The study of the authority of an erroneous conscience occurs in Question Nineteen, which deals with the moral appraisal of acts of the will. The first two articles argue that the will is to be judged good simply according as the object a man wills is good. The third article makes this a little more precise: "the

[1] Gilson places the date of the *Prima Secundae* as some time after January, 1269. (*Christian Philosophy of St. Thomas Aquinas*, p. 387.)

object of the will" is the object as seen, judged
and presented by the reason, and so the moral
appraisal of the will is to be made in the light
of the judgement presented to it by the reason;
this is the principle originally put forward in
the *Commentary on the Sentences*. This brings
us to our question. The reason may be mistaken
in its judgement of a moral situation—that is,
conscience may err. Supposing that a man acts
against this erroneous conscience, his action may
yet prove to have been in harmony with objective morality; he has reached the right answer
by wrong calculation. On the other hand, a man
may follow his conscience, and faithfully do
what he (mistakenly) believes to be right. What
should we think of these actions? Articles Five
and Six consider these issues.

The title of Article Five is "If reason be in
error, is the will evil by being at variance with
it?" St. Thomas remarks immediately that it is
the same thing to ask this question as to ask, "Is
an erroneous conscience binding?" For conscience is a command of the reason applying
moral principles to a proposed act.

He quotes the view which, as we have seen,
was the general opinion of the thirteenth-
century moralists, especially Secular and Franciscan masters: an erroneous conscience is
binding in matters which are morally indifferent, but not in matters which are good or

evil by their nature. Once again he rejects this in the light of the principle propounded in the *Commentary on the Sentences*, and repeated in an earlier part of the present question: the reason may present things that are objectively indifferent as good or as evil, things that are objectively good as evil, or things that are objectively evil as good; but the will is to be judged in all these cases according to the standard of the-object-as-presented-by-the-reason. There is therefore, Aquinas claims, no ground for the distinction made in the theory of his contemporaries. He then puts down his own final position:

> The object of the will is that which is presented to it by the reason. Therefore, by the very fact that something is presented by the reason as evil, the will in pursuing it incurs guilt.

He gives two rather striking examples. It is virtuous to refrain from fornication; but if for some reason a man believes that such abstinence is sinful, he sins by so abstaining. Again, belief in Christ is good and salutary; but if a man sincerely, though mistakenly, judges it to be evil, he would sin by embracing the Christian faith. "His will is evil because it wills evil", not evil in itself, but evil by the will's own proper standard, which is the appraisal made by the reason. He paraphrases Aristotle:

> Essentially, a man is incontinent if he does not follow right reason; but accidentally, also if he does not follow false reason.

So his conclusion is absolute:

> We must therefore hold, without qualification, that whether the reason be correct or mistaken, the will which is at variance with it is always evil.

The interesting objection is that in which the Emperor-and-proconsul parallel is invoked. Augustine says that the precept of a lower authority, such as a proconsul, does not bind against a contrary ordinance given by his superior, such as the Emperor; but an erroneous conscience is subordinate to God, and runs counter to his ordinance; hence it cannot be binding. St. Thomas' answer this time is crisp, and seems to be simple common sense. St. Augustine's principle would be relevant *if one knew* that the subordinate's command ran counter to his superior's; but if a person believed that the proconsul's precept was the Emperor's precept, then to defy the proconsul's precept would be to defy the Emperor's. So it is when a person's conscience presents something as God's command. For that person, to scorn the dictate of conscience is to scorn the command of God.

Article Six takes up the obverse question: If you do follow a misguided conscience, is your action therefore good? Here we find St. Thomas applying to the question his theory of invincible ignorance, and so being led to modify the strict position he adopted in the *De Veritate*. We have already noticed that in the *Commentary on the Sentences* St. Thomas failed to make any connection between the questions of ignorance and of erroneous conscience, and that in the *De Veritate* the connection was used but not elaborated. But in the *Summa*, the issue of invincible ignorance is invoked as the basic principle relevant to the solution. The point is not whether conscience is mistaken about a matter of law or a matter of fact, but whether the mistake is blameworthy or not.

He begins by claiming that, just as the last question was the same as the query "Does an erroneous conscience *bind*?" the present is the same as the query "Does an erroneous conscience *excuse*?" He says that this depends on an earlier discussion[1] of the effect of ignorance on voluntariety, which he recalls. Some ignorance renders an act non-voluntary, some does not. But an act

[1] *ST*, 1–2,6,8.

is morally good or evil only in so far as it is voluntary. So the first principle is reached:

> When ignorance is such as to render an action non-voluntary it takes from it the status of being morally good or bad; not so, however, when it does not render the action non-voluntary.

Now, when ignorance is itself voluntary in any way, Aquinas claims that it does not render the ensuing action non-voluntary. This may occur in two ways. First, a man may intend precisely to be in ignorance, either in order to have some excuse to plead for his wrongdoing, or so as not to be deterred from it. Second, ignorance is also voluntary in the relevant sense when it concerns things which he is both able and obliged to know; either because through passion or force of habit he does not advert to duties he knows quite well; or because he does not bother to inform himself of, for example, general principles of the law. In all such cases, Aquinas holds, moral responsibility is still to be ascribed to the action which arises out of ignorance. He concludes, then, that when conscience is erroneous in either of these ways, the man who follows his conscience is guilty and culpable.

On the other hand, the error made by con-

science may be completely blameless. This
occurs when there is some factual circumstance
of which the agent is ignorant, and there is no
question of negligence. In such cases, Aquinas
holds, the man's erroneous conscience excuses
him, and his will in following conscience is not
guilty of evil.

In the terms of this distinction he answers a
case in point: What if a man's guilty conscience
mistakenly tells him that he is obliged to have
intercourse with another man's wife? If the
mistake concerns the divine law against adultery,
he is not excused, for a man is bound to know
the law of God. But, says Aquinas, his mistake
may consist in thinking that the woman in
question is his own wife, although in reality she
is another man's. In that case he is excused from
sin, since the error arises from ignorance of a
factual circumstance which rendered the act involuntary under the relevant description. (An
unusual enough situation, one may imagine, for
no touch of negligence to be involved.)

St. Thomas is now in a better position to deal
with the case of the moral dilemma, which he
presents as follows: It has been held that it is
sinful to act against a misguided conscience. If
it is now held that it is sinful also to follow it,
then a man sins whatever he does—an insup-
portable view. Given the distinction with which
the solution was offered, the way is now clear;

by definition, it is sinful to follow a mistaken conscience only when the mistake is voluntary, and obviously there is nothing to prevent a man from shedding a voluntarily erroneous conscience.

3. THE CASE COMPLETED

SO much by way of stating St. Thomas'
views. They were revolutionary, and their
basic principles are permanently valid; we
shall be indebted to them throughout this essay.
But on some scores his account seems to be
defective. If we can set them right we shall be
in a strong position to argue the case for the
right to freedom of conscience.

1. "Not Bad" or "Good"?

I want to suggest that, in both these articles
in the *Summa*, St. Thomas has not carried his
own principle to its logical conclusion.

In Article Five, he bases his case on the
principle, "The object of the will is that which
is presented to it by the reason": that is, an
object is not what that which is pursued is in
reality, but what the agent believes it to be.
This leads St. Thomas to the negative conclusion: "One is always bound not to act against
conscience"; as his principle entails. But he
fights shy of drawing the positive conclusion,
"One is always bound to follow one's conscience." This seems to be equally entailed by
his principle wherever one's conscience has been

formed in good faith. Father Copleston shows what the conclusion should be:

> If our conscience tells us that we ought to perform a particular act, it is our moral duty to perform it.[1]

This certainly should be Aquinas' conclusion, but in fact he draws it only with the restriction, "in such a way that, if a person acts against his conscience, he sins".[2]

Article Six seems to be similarly defective. We should expect the conclusion, "Any action which follows conscience is praiseworthy and good." But the most that is conceded in the case of an erroneous conscience is that the action which it commends may be excused from blame, not bad.

That this is St. Thomas' maximum concession seems clear for five reasons. First, the preliminary objections in an article in the *Summa* are always directed *against* St. Thomas' own view; and in this article, each of the objections concludes with the words, "Therefore even when the reason is in error, the will is good if it follows it." Second, the *sed contra* always espouses the view which he wishes to defend; and in this article it concludes, "Therefore the will can be evil, even when it follows reason." This may be

[1] *Aquinas*, Penguin, 1955, p. 220.
[2] *Quodlib.*, 3,27, which Copleston quotes.

compatible with the view that the will may
sometimes be exonerated from guilt, but hardly
with holding that it is positively good. Third,
the actual argument in the body of the article
seems only to reach the point that such action
may be non-voluntary and hence, at best, neither
good nor bad, not a candidate for moral appraisal
at all. Fourth, St. Thomas nowhere states as a
conclusion that the act is good, but only that it
may be excused from the verdict of being bad.
Fifth, the reply to the first objection seems to
clinch the matter. For an action to be bad, *either*
of two conditions is *sufficient*: that the action
really is bad, or that it is believed to be bad.
But for an action to be good, *each* of two conditions is *necessary*: that the action really is
good, and that it is believed to be good. The
conclusion therefore seems clear: the maximum
concession that St. Thomas will make is that an
action which follows an erroneous conscience
may sometimes be non-voluntary, and hence
without any moral status, blameless, not bad; he
denies that such an action can be praiseworthy
or good. I now want to suggest that in this he is
not consistent.

His own principle is: The object of the will,
and therefore the criterion of moral good or evil,
is the good, not as it is in itself, but as it is presented by the intellect. Now, in the case we are
considering, the action is in conformity with this

criterion, and by hypothesis the error of conscience has been made in good faith. Only one conclusion seems possible: the action has faithfully measured up to its own standard, and so is to be adjudged good.

Perhaps the point may be made more clearly if we first clear St. Thomas of another charge of apparent inconsistency. In Article Three of this, Question Nineteen, he holds that the goodness of the human will depends solely on its object, and in no way on circumstances external to the act. Yet in the previous question[1] he held that the goodness or evil of a human action does not depend on its object alone, but on its circumstances and the agent's purpose as well. This point is familiar enough. To be under a strong temptation or urge to commit murder, and then to refuse oneself a ready opportunity to do so, seems to be a praiseworthy forbearance, or at least a morally good and dutiful decision. But in the case of Hamlet's deciding not to kill the King at prayer, it was thoroughly base, because prompted by a motive more wicked than that of murder[2]; he resolved to wait until he could take his uncle in an act that had no relish of salvation in it, and send his soul to hell. In assessing the morality of a given action, all three factors are relevant: the object of the action, the purpose

[1] Q. 18, arts. 2,3,4.
[2] As the Bishop of Galway has pointed out.

of the agent, and the circumstances of the performance.

Why, then, in the present Question Nineteen, does he say that the only relevant factor is the object? Because in the previous article he was studying the general criteria for pronouncing a human action good or bad, that is, the conditions which must be fulfilled before we can pronounce an action good *sans plus*. But in the present article he is studying the criteria by which we are to assess the interior performance of the human will. It is quite common for us to pronounce one and the same situation as good in the latter sense but not in the former. For the word "object" has two quite different senses in these questions. In Question Eighteen it means simply the act under its natural description; thus the action described as "almsgiving" has an identical *object* whether the donor's *purpose* was to alleviate misery, to win votes, or to bribe the beggar to commit a crime. But in Question Nineteen the word "object" refers to the total complex pursued by the will, and this, as Aquinas says, will include both the end and the object in the senses in which they were used in the previous question.

But this is merely to arouse again the charge of inconsistency against St. Thomas. The will has only one way of recognizing good or evil: the picture presented to it by reason. If reason presents a false picture, the will cannot be blamed; there is only one standard for judging it: the good as apprehended. If it fails to live up to that, its only standard, its performance is bad. But if it is faithful to its only standard, its performance is surely good. What else is a standard for?

Now, an attempt might be made to clear St. Thomas of the charge of inconsistency along other lines. Perhaps when he says that the object of the will is the good as apprehended by the reason, he is referring to the picture it presents of the facts, not its moral appraisal of the facts. Think of the cases he gives. If a man shoots his father under the impression that his target is a stag, he is not to be deemed guilty of parricide. If a man has intercourse with another man's wife under the impression that she is his own wife, he is not to be deemed guilty of adultery.

But surely this is not a tenable account of his meaning. Constantly he uses such phrases as, "If it be apprehended by the reason as evil", "If it be proposed by the intellect as good." Such phrases cannot be restricted to factual observations, but must apply to value-judgements as well. Furthermore, the examples given in Article Five are cases of errors in matters of principle, and not merely of fact: one is the person who believes that faith in Christ is sinful, the other the person who believes it wrong to abstain from committing fornication. I think that words written in another context by Miss Anscombe would translate the criterion in question quite accurately:

> The notion of "good" that has to be introduced in an account of wanting is not that of what is really good, but of what the agent conceives to be good.[1]

Finally, one may remark that even where the judgement of the reason is mistaken only in a matter of fact, St. Thomas will not say the act is good. He is prepared to go no further than styling it non-voluntary, and so without moral status and, as such, not evil. Yet here certainly the will is conforming to the standard he assigns it: the faithful adherence of a man's will to the good as he sees the good.

The point could have been made more directly. The body of the article opened by saying that the question, "If the reason be in error, is the will in following it thereby good?" is identical with the question, "Does an erroneous conscience excuse?" He closes it with the conclusion that, in certain circumstances, the answer to the second question is, "Yes." Logically then, in the same circumstances, the answer to the first question should be, "Yes." And indeed, it looks as if St. Thomas felt un-

[1] *Intention*, p. 76.

comfortable about his position, for the conclusion repeats the heading of the article verbatim until the last word: (... in such circumstances) "if the reason be in error, the will in following it is thereby *not bad*."

Père Olivier suggests that this article is inconsistent on another score[1]; but his argument seems to be not quite sound. He recalls St. Thomas' principle that, whereas some *types* of act may be morally indifferent in the abstract, any given *individual* act in the concrete is either good or evil.[2] He concludes, "If therefore an act that is imposed wrongly by an invincibly faulty conscience is not a sin, in concrete fact it cannot be anything but a good act." But this appears to miss the point of St. Thomas' answer. His contention that every individual act is either good or evil applies only to acts which are fully voluntary, "the product of rational deliberation". But in the article on the erroneous conscience, he excuses the act precisely on the grounds that ignorance renders the act non-voluntary. We have found some difficulty about this explanation, but it seems to clear St. Thomas of this particular charge of inconsistency.

Let us now see how the work which St.

[1] B. Olivier, "The Rights of Conscience", in *Tolerance and the Catholic*, trans. G. Lamb, New York, Sheed and Ward, 1955, p. 148, *n*. 7.
[2] *ST*, 1–2,18,9.

Thomas pioneered has been completed, and the supremacy of a conscience formed in good faith fully recognized, by modern Catholic moralists. The chapter on conscience is an important one in any modern Catholic work on moral science, and the clarity of the present day is largely indebted to the controversies of the seventeenth and eighteenth centuries concerning conscience. They were not primarily concerned with the claims of true and false conscience, but with the claims of certain or doubtful conscience. But they resulted in a great precision in formulating the basic principles of the authority of conscience, and the full conclusions are drawn of which St. Thomas fought shy. There are two problems to be noticed.

First, the supreme authority of conscience is recognized, not only in the negative sense that one is forbidden to act against it, but also in the positive sense that one is obliged to follow it: provided, of course, that one's conscience is formed in good faith. There is no need for us to retrace the arguments, since they merely carry St. Thomas' principles to their logical conclusion. It may be of value to illustrate the attitude of modern Catholic moralists by quoting from two manuals which are commonly used as textbooks in seminaries training men for the priesthood. Vermeersch writes as follows:

Conscience is the immediate criterion of morality. In one sense, an action has its remote criterion in the law; but in quite a different way, it finds its immediate criterion in conscience ... One is always bound to follow conscience when it feels certain about its immediate duty.[1]

And Genicot:

When conscience feels certain, whether it be correct or mistaken, one is always obliged to follow it when it enjoins or forbids; and one is always entitled to follow it, when it recommends or permits.[2]

Such writers insist, of course, on the duty to take all reasonable care that one's conscience is correctly formed; but given that the judgement of conscience has been formed in good faith, one is obliged to follow it. It is interesting to compare these statements with those of two moralists very far from the scholastic tradition. In the late eighteenth century Reid wrote:

Morality requires, not only that a man should act according to his judgement, but that he should use the best means in his power that

[1] *Theologiae Moralis Principia*, Rome, 1923, vol. 1, pp. 290, 293.

[2] *Institutiones Theologiae Moralis*, Brussels, Desclée, 1931, vol. 1, p. 42.

the judgement be according to truth. If he fail in either of these points, he is worthy of blame; but, if he fail in neither, I see not where he can be blamed.[1]

And in our own day Professor Baier has written:

... "Ought he to do the subjectively or the objectively right act?" This question can perplex us only because we have no more than a confused understanding of its sense. As soon as we make clear to ourselves the various different things it can mean, the problem vanishes. If we mean "Does thinking that something is one's duty make it so?" the answer is obviously "No". If we mean "Does the moral man do what after careful consideration he has worked out to be what he ought to do?" the answer is, of course, "Yes". If it means "Should a person who has worked out what he ought to do as carefully and conscientiously as can be expected be rebuked for acting on his results?" the answer is plainly "No". If it means "Is a man ever to be rebuked for doing what he thought he ought to do?" the answer is, of course, "Yes, sometimes, for he may culpably have failed in his theoretical task."[2]

[1] "Essays on the Active Powers", 2, in the *Works*, Edinburgh, 1863, vol. 2, p. 647.

[2] K. Baier, *The Moral Point of View*, Ithaca, Cornell University Press, 1958, pp. 146–7.

Second, it is recognized that an action is formally good[1] if it is done in accordance with conscience. This is true whether the judgement of conscience is objectively correct or erroneous; the only condition is that it has been reached in good faith. About the year 1750 St. Alphonsus saw that this was the logical outcome of St. Thomas' principle, and since then most Catholic moralists have felt that his argument cannot be gainsaid. Prümmer[2] mentions only Concinna as having demurred at the argument in the two hundred years since it was stated.

As the basis of his case, Alphonsus[3] chose words of Aquinas which are very telling indeed:

A human act is judged to be virtuous or vicious by the standard of the good as it has been apprehended, which is what the will pursues; and not by the standard of the action's material object.[4]

It is a shrewd choice. St. Thomas was willing to deduce from this principle that the action which runs counter to conscience is bad; he was not

[1] This is not to say that it is supernaturally meritorious. That an action be morally good, at least formally, is a necessary, but not a sufficient, condition of its being supernaturally meritorious.

[2] *Manuale Theologiae Moralis*, Fribourg, Herder, 1958, vol. 1, p. 195.

[3] *Theologia Moralis*, Rome, 1912, vol. 1, 6.

[4] *Quodlib.*, 3,27.

ready to deduce that the action which follows it is good. Yet here are his own words for it that the good as apprehended, i.e., the judgement of conscience, is the standard of virtue as well as of vice. So the following statement of Vermeersch is typical of Catholic opinion today:

> One is always bound to follow conscience when it feels certain about its immediate duty . . . Hence, whether in theory conscience be correct or mistaken, an action will have in fact whatever evil or goodness conscience attributes to it.[1]

Following another lead from St. Thomas, the modern writers give an account of the phrase, "Conscience is the voice of God." Genicot takes up St. Thomas' treatment of Augustine's parallel of the Emperor-and-proconsul. From it St. Thomas drew only the negative conclusion that it is the same thing to despise the command of conscience as to despise the command of God. Genicot takes the argument to the positive conclusion that it is the same thing to obey the command of conscience as to obey the command of God.

> As far as a given action is concerned, an erroneous conscience is binding in exactly the same way as is a correct one. Provided it be

[1] Vol. 1, p. 293.

certain, an erroneous conscience shows a man what is God's will in exactly the same way as does a correct one.[1]

2. IGNORANCE OF THE LAW

Through these discussions, we have constantly encountered one proviso: it is obligatory and good to follow conscience, always provided that one has formed that conscience in good faith. Now, this suggests a possible way out of the criticism that St. Thomas has not carried his principles to their logical conclusion; if he could show that ignorance of fact is the only possible source of inculpably erroneous conscience, all would be well with his account. But in this he was never completely happy. We have seen that St. Thomas wavered somewhat concerning the possibility of inculpable ignorance. In the *De Veritate* he appeared to hold that ignorance about facts could be blameless but ignorance of law or principle could not. In the *De Malo* he recognized that ignorance of either might be blameless. In these articles in the *Summa* he seems to move back towards his first position.

The trouble seems to arise from making the distinction at the wrong point. As far as the *object* of ignorance is concerned, we may make a threefold distinction: there may be ignorance

[1] Vol. 1, p. 42.

of a relevant fact, ignorance of principle or law, and ignorance of sanction or punishment. But in terms of the *subject* who is ignorant, the relevant distinction will be simply twofold, corrigible or incorrigible. Ignorance may be incorrigible because it never occurred to me that there was some important fact to be investigated; or because it has never occurred to me to question my own principles, since they are commonly held in the society where I live; or because background or upbringing has conditioned me to disparage the intelligence, the sincerity, or even the social status of those who challenge these principles.

Now, it would seem that in assessing the bearing of ignorance upon moral responsibility, it is the *subjective* factor which will be relevant. It would appear that, in considering the matter in terms of the *objective* factor, St. Thomas is tackling the problem at the wrong point. The question is not whether my ignorance or my mistake concerned a point of fact or a point of law, but whether or not it was corrigible in the relevant sense. Even if it were so corrigible, my personal guilt will be measured, not by the damage that in fact results from it, but by the degree of my culpability in labouring under such error. Where ignorance is not corrigible, then, in the sense described, the conclusion will be absolute: incorrigible ignorance, whether it concern a point of fact or a point of principle, exonerates a man completely.

Of course, this does not mean that his action is objectively good. To recognize that a man deserves well if he is faithful in following sincere judgements of conscience is not to condone a theory of moral relativism. After all, the Thomist conceives his ethic as part of the large metaphysic of potentiality and act. "Natural law" is a Janus-term. In so far as it is *natural*, it describes those types of action which will in fact fulfil, "actual-ize", the real, though yet unfulfilled, potenti-alities of human nature. Whether a man be in good faith or not, a given act either will in fact contribute to this actualization, or it will frus-trate it. If it frustrates, it is objectively bad. It is therefore proper, given the right circum-stances, to challenge moral principles one believes to be objectively wrong, that is, inimical to human fulfilment. Such considera-tions are prompted by the "natural" element in natural-law theory.

But natural law is also *law*, and no man is under formal responsibility to obey a law except in so far as he knows it. Our concern in this chapter has been to study a man's subjective responsibility, his personal culpability or blame-lessness, the ground of his merit or demerit; and our conclusion is clear. Provided there has been no culpable neglect in forming conscience, the

action which follows it is subjectively good, and
the action which runs counter to it is subjectively
bad. The formal morality of an action is to be
measured entirely in terms of the dictate of
conscience at the moment of its performance.
Whether, objectively speaking, that dictate be
correct or mistaken, the action will have in fact
whatever goodness or evil conscience attributes
to it.

With all this St. Thomas might agree—in
principle. Certainly, he might say, all that you
say is quite true—provided that there has been
no culpable negligence in forming one's conscience. But this is exactly what cannot be. For
in the cases you envisage, there will always be
an "error in a matter which we are both able
and obliged to know". This seems to be the
other defect in Article Six; the phrase is an
obscure one, and St. Thomas does not eluci-
date it.

It reminds one of Nowell-Smith's remark that
the man who adopts and adheres to bad moral
principles is wicked; whereas the man who has
good moral principles but fails to live up to
them is morally weak[1]; this in turn is reminis-
cent of Aristotle:

Every wicked man is ignorant of what he
ought to do and what he ought to abstain

[1] P. H. Nowell-Smith, *Ethics*, Penguin, 1954, p. 265.

from, and it is by reason of error of this kind that men become unjust and in general bad.[1]

Such remarks raise a serious difficulty against the case we have just been making. Apparently Himmler thought it wrong for him not to kill Jews. Does that mean it was right for him not to do so? No, says Nowell-Smith; he was a wicked man for holding such a principle. No, says Miss Anscombe: "Butler too exalts conscience, but appears ignorant that a man's conscience may tell him to do the vilest things."[2] No, says St. Thomas; he was mistaken in a matter which he was both obliged and able to correct.

An intimidating chorus. But suppose that the question concerns, not the killing of Jewish people, but killing an unborn child in order to save its mother's life. I believe that such an action is unjust and murderous; but I do not consider the man who disagrees with me *wicked*; I think that he is mistaken, often in the utmost good faith. During the nineteenth century a few Catholic moral theologians, including the influential Ballerini, thought that in these circumstances abortion was permissible. It was not that their mistake concerned only a matter of fact— say, that for some months the foetus was not a

[1] *Nicomachean Ethics*, 1110 b, 27-30 (Ross's translation).

[2] "Modern Moral Philosophy", in *Philosophy*, Jan. 1958, p. 2.

human being; it concerned a matter of moral principle. They argued, for instance, that one should choose the lesser of two evils; but to perform an abortion means that the child alone will die; whereas not to perform it often means that both mother and child will die. Again, they argued that the child is in the same case as an unjust aggressor; and it is lawful to cause the death of an unjust aggressor if there is no other way of saving the innocent life which he is threatening. The flaws in these arguments were soon exposed; but one does not say that, during the years these theologians held and presented this view, they were wicked. Their mistake was not one of fact. It was a principle which they held, which I believe to be immoral. Many people sincerely hold the same view today and act on it. It is good to argue with them, to contest their view, to challenge their reasons. But I refuse to call them wicked.

To deal with this soundly, then, St. Thomas would need to give a coherent account of his phrase, "Error in matters we are both able and obliged to know." We have already found it difficult to know just how this is to be understood. We found that in the *De Malo* he altered his earlier views, and admitted that there can be inculpable error or ignorance in questions of principle or law as well as in matters of fact. But in this place in the *Summa* he seems to return to the view that every mistake concerning the law of God is culpable, since we are bound to know it. What exactly does this mean? Does it refer to the primary or secondary precepts of the moral law, or, even further, to divine positive law? Then, to whom does it apply? To the Christian faithful? Or to all adults?

Most important, how would St. Thomas reconcile this position with his own principle, "No-one is bound by a law save by one means only: knowledge of that law"? On that count, it would not be enough for him to say that we are *bound* not to be ignorant of the moral law; in the light of this principle he must show that we are *unable* to be ignorant of it. And at what level of logical particularity is that true?

The fact is that it seems an oversimplification to say that errors concerning moral questions are either errors about law or errors about fact. In three other places of the *Summa* St. Thomas shows himself very much alive to the complexity of moral situations.

In the *Prima Secundae*, in the treatise on law, he studies the extent to which the eternal law is known to all men; and he concludes that all men know the general precepts of the natural law, but that, as these become more particular, some men know more of them and some less.[1] This becomes clearer when he studies the extent to

[1] 93,2.

which the natural law is known to all men.[1]
There are some precepts which all adults necessarily know, and some which cannot be unknown
without personal fault. But the more we par-
ticularize the very general precepts, the more
likely we are to err; and long before we reach
the level of the concrete, individual case there
is room for *bona fide* disagreements. Here St.
Thomas is simply recapitulating what he wrote
in his commentary on the *Nicomachean Ethics*:

> First and foremost, morality is concerned with
> virtuous or righteous deeds ... Human beings
> have no certainty concerning these things, and
> differ greatly in their opinions about them,
> and many mistakes occur. Some men hold
> certain things to be right and good which are
> deemed by men of other times or places or
> character to be wrong and wicked. The very
> same thing is held at one time or in one
> country to be wicked which, at another time
> or in another country, is not thought to be
> wrong at all.[2]

St. Thomas had very little anthropological data
on which to work, but there is nothing in, say,
Professor Brandt's book *Hopi Ethics* which need
have embarrassed him. Nor are moral disagreements and uncertainty confined to primitive

[1] 94,2 and 4.
[2] *In I Eth.*, l. 3.

peoples, or the man in the street; they have always existed even among the most skilled moralists. This becomes all the clearer to us when we look through any volume of writing on morals and see the plethora of disputed questions; or when we see Ross trying to draw up a list of *"prima facie* duties" according to priorities of obligation. Ballerini's is but one chastening example out of hundreds.

In the *Secunda Secundae*, the treatise on practical wisdom, *prudentia*,[1] St. Thomas again shows a lively awareness of the complexity of moral situations. The good moral life can never consist solely in robot-like obedience to the directives of bishops and statesmen. It is quite impossible that all decisions be made in advance for man by law, whether divine or human, natural or positive. There will always be, in moral conduct, a wide field of particular decisions to be made by each man freely and responsibly under the law. The application of the general law in a given situation calls, therefore, for a high degree of skill, so that practical wisdom is styled "the moderator of the other virtues". St. Thomas' analysis of it discovers eight constitutive qualities,[2] and calls for three distinct acts in its successful operation.[3]

[1] Qq. 47–51.
[2] Q. 49, arts. 1–8.
[3] Q. 47, art. 8.

Looking forward to such complexities, the *Pars Prima*, in dealing with synderesis and conscience,[1] had found St. Thomas alive to many possible sources of error in the judgements of conscience. This we have seen already. Earlier still, St. Thomas had devoted a whole article[2] to the possible sources of erroneous judgement of conscience, setting out four major sources.

Even the most enthusiastic Thomists admit that St. Thomas failed to give an adequate account of the connection between practical wisdom and conscience.[3] Our point here is simply to remark that, for want of such an account, a lacuna exists in the article on the authority of erroneous conscience, and we are left with the rather vague principle that such a conscience grants indemnity only when the error concerns matters we have no duty to know.

The weakness is the more surprising when we recall the precisions made in the *De Malo* as compared with the *De Veritate*. In the *De Veritate* we were given the black-and-white distinction that blameless error is possible in matters of fact, but on matters of law error is always culpable. We might say that before the

[1] 79,12–13.

[2] *De Ver.*, q. 17, art. 2.

[3] e.g., Deman, *Traduction française de la Somme théologique: La Prudence*, Paris, Desclée, 1932, pp. 496–511.

De Malo St. Thomas was in a position similar to that of Nowell-Smith: the man who fails to follow right principles is morally weak, but the man who holds wrong moral principles is wicked. In the *De Malo*, and in the *Summa*'s treatises on prudence and law, St. Thomas found that this was an oversimplification. But in the articles on the authority of conscience he does not invoke the refinements which he had introduced in these other places.

Perhaps no-one can hope to determine in detail the extent to which ignorance of the moral law is possible. But on three points modern Catholic accounts represent some advance on St. Thomas'. First, they have at their disposal the data of modern social anthropology, with its copious reports of the moral values and principles which peoples of different cultures, times and places have actually held. Such reports discourage any attempt to state dogmatically, on aprioristic grounds, precisely what ethical rules and values "must" be known to all human beings. Second, it is commonly recognized that blameless ignorance of law or moral principle often exists, simply because it has never occurred to a person to question his principles. This is all the more likely when faulty moral standards are fairly widespread in a community. We may deplore the prevalence of views that we believe to be objectively wrong, and we may challenge them. But we should be slow to attribute bad faith to people who have never had occasion to call such views in question, or suffer some psychological blockage, whether of upbringing or heredity, which prevents their entering into such discussions with an open mind, whether they concern professional or business ethics, private or family morality. Furthermore, modern scholastics agree that it is quite difficult to say which are the "common principles of the natural law" given by "innate habit" to every man; and harder still to say which are the immediate deductions from them. Vermeersch[1] remarks that positive laws (of God, or human authority) may certainly be the subject of blameless ignorance, as also the more remote conclusions of the natural (moral) law. He thinks that the immediate conclusions may not; and becomes increasingly hesitant as he attempts to specify what these are. He mentions, presumably with decreasing confidence, homicide, adultery, masturbation, contraception.

His hesitance is surely the product of wisdom. It is often not acumen nor realism, but sheer lack of experience which prompts such brash pronouncements as, "These people really know in their hearts that their views are wrong." Without altering scholastic terminology, we can

[1] Vol. 1, p. 71.

see that there are many sources of erroneous conscience; ignorance of positive law, remote conclusions of natural law, and even some not so remote: inadvertence to the need to examine one's principles; defect of practical wisdom in choosing the relevant principle or applying it to the case in hand; and error concerning matters of fact.

Contra factum non valet dialectica. St. Thomas was the last person to push *a-priori* argument in the face of facts. He was handicapped by not having very much information about the moral values of peoples beyond the borders of Christendom; but he readily accepted what tenuous information was available, and incorporated it in his theory: for example, Julius Caesar's report that the Germans did not look on robbery as immoral, "even though it is in fact expressly against the law of nature". Nowadays we have a great deal more information concerning the ethical beliefs of primitive peoples, and of pagans of high cultural achievement. We have first-hand knowledge of the change induced in the moral values of a community once Christian when Christianity ceases to be a determining factor in shaping its values. It is therefore distressing to hear such remarks as, "Mohammedans really know that polygamy is wicked"; "Pre-Wilberforce politicians knew quite well that condoning slavery was wrong"; "People who defend birth-control are not sincere; they know in their hearts that it is immoral."

Theologians are helped in their approach to the problem by St. Paul's remarks in the first two chapters of the Epistle to the Romans. But for them, too, there is a residual problem of meaning, as the endless exegesis of the passages show. At what level of generality did St. Paul mean that moral ignorance is always culpable? The question has been studied with a wealth of care, subtlety and detail quite beyond the scope of the present work even to summarize; but it is possible to indicate the *point de départ*. Theologians have tended to take what the Vatican Council taught concerning the knowledge of *natural* religious truths and apply it, *mutatis mutandis*, to knowledge of moral matters: without divine revelation it is morally (though not absolutely) impossible for most men, given the present condition of the human race, to arrive at such knowledge with certainty, accuracy, and "no admixture of error". Father Copleston's words reflect this trend:

> Since the influence of passion and of inclinations which are not in accordance with right reason may lead men astray and since not all men have the time or ability or patience to discover the whole natural law for themselves,

it was morally necessary that the natural law should be positively expressed by God, as was done by the revelation of the Decalogue to Moses.[1]

It may be impossible to be blamelessly ignorant that murder is wrong; but suppose one has been brought by one's tribe to believe that to kill another tribesman is not murder, but a proof of one's manhood? At one stage St. Augustine was inclined to wonder whether, in certain circumstances, a woman might be morally obliged to commit adultery, given her husband's consent.

Such points raise again the problems considered at the end of our first chapter, and we still have found no detailed solution for them. Fortunately, however, this element of indecision does not crucially affect the central theme of this book. We are concerned with the right to freedom of conscience only in matters of religious choice, profession and worship; and in these matters blameless ignorance may occur much more easily than in questions of morality. For, in Thomist theory, moral rules are derived from basic principles which are "engraved", in some way, in the very nature of man; whereas religious truth, where supernatural revelation is in question, is often information about the inner

[1] *A History of Philosophy*, London, Burns, Oates and Washbourne, 1959, vol. 2, p. 409.

life of God himself. Pope Pius V condemned Michael de Bay's proposition, "Purely negative unbelief, in people to whom Christ has not been preached, is a sin." De Bay's opinion would sound even more peculiar today when so many people hear of religion with a mixture of apathy, antipathy and ignorance.

At all events, the arguments appear to have led us to the conclusions expressed, as we have seen, by modern moral theologians in such phrases as:

> One is always bound to follow conscience whenever it enjoins or forbids ... As far as a given action is concerned, an erroneous conscience is binding in exactly the same way as is a correct one ... Whether in theory conscience be correct or mistaken, an action will have in fact whatever evil or goodness conscience attributes to it ... Provided it be certain, an erroneous conscience shows a man what is God's will for him, in exactly the same way as does a correct one.

It is on these principles that we may expect the case for the right to freedom of conscience to be based.

PART III

PART III

THE BREAKDOWN OF THE ARGUMENT: ST. THOMAS ON RELIGIOUS FREEDOM

IT has come to be expected that a person who holds for the moral authority of conscience will also hold for the individual's freedom to follow his conscience without interference from the State. This essay is interested specifically in that aspect of the question of freedom of conscience which concerns religious choice, profession and worship. Our next step, then, is to inquire into St. Thomas' views regarding the freedoms to which religious dissenters are entitled. But in pursuing the inquiry, this chapter sets itself a limited objective; it attempts no general appraisal of St. Thomas' treatment of the subject, but is primarily concerned with it in connection with his account of the concept and authority of conscience.

The relevant articles in the *Summa Theologica* are found in the questions which study "unbelief". The *Secunda Secundae* opens with the treatise on the theological virtue of faith, and within this treatise three questions are devoted to matters concerning unbelievers; five of the articles deal with the freedoms to which they are entitled. St. Thomas' order of treatment will not be the most convenient for our own purpose; his Question Ten studies matters concerning unbelievers in general, by which he means simply people who are not Catholics, whether they once belonged to the Church or not; questions eleven and twelve deal with those people only who once were Catholics and have fallen into heresy or apostasy. An arrangement more suitable here will be to take, first, the places in which St. Thomas advocates freedom for unbelievers, and second, the places in which he opposes it.

A word must be said concerning the translation of St. Thomas' term *infidelis*, which is here rendered "unbeliever". The English "infidel" seems unsuitable, since it usually carries with it a suggestion of an antipathy to Christianity; it is more strongly perjorative than, say, the Latin *infidelis* in the Code of Canon Law, which, unlike St. Thomas, reserves the term for one who has never received Christian baptism in any denomination. The term *fideles*, both in St. Thomas' writing and in ordinary Catholic usage, is used as a synonym for "Catholics", members of the Church; St. Thomas accordingly uses the term *infidelis* for any person who is not a Catholic, whether he is a Christian or not. It would therefore be accurate to translate "non-Catholic"; but this is not only a cumbersome term, but also, to many people, savours of complacency, or even of a kind of religious chauvinism. Perhaps, then, the least unsatisfactory rendering will be "unbeliever"; but it is important to remember that, in St. Thomas' writings, the term does not bear the literal meaning suggested by the word, nor its meaning in modern Catholic usage, but simply connotes "one who is not a Catholic".

1. ST. THOMAS AS THE ADVOCATE OF FREEDOM

St. Thomas holds that there are two freedoms to which unbelievers are strictly entitled: for parents, he claims the right to decide their children's religious affiliation; and for those who have never been Catholics, freedom from all coercive pressure to enter the Church.

1. THE RIGHTS OF PARENTS

In the treatise on faith St. Thomas devotes an article to the rights of parents concerning their children's religion. He holds without qualification that it is never permissible to give Christian baptism to the children of Jews or other unbelievers against their parents' wishes; first, because this would be a violation of natural justice; second, because it would do harm to the Christian faith. The issue is taken up again in an article in the treatise on baptism, where two points which had been broached in the earlier article are amplified. These two articles provide us with some valuable principles, and indicate effective lines of reply to some arguments, still raised even in our own time, against the right to religious freedom.

St. Thomas begins[1] by remarking that the Church has never countenanced the baptism of the children of Jews or other unbelievers against their parents' wishes. Through the centuries, he says, many powerful Catholic princes have heeded the advice of saintly bishops; these bishops would certainly have urged such a measure had it been in keeping with sound reason, but they never did so. From the point of view of tradition, then, it would be most unhealthy to introduce such a novelty; and from the point of view of the Faith, too. For when such children reached the age of discretion, their parents would easily persuade them to abandon what they had received all unaware; indeed their natural affection for their parents would incline them so to act.[2] Their falling-away would then certainly do harm to the general fervour of the Faith.

After these considerations of religious well-

[1] *ST*, 2–2,10,12c.
[2] This remark occurs in the article in the treatise on baptism, *ST*, 3,68,10.

being and ecclesiastical policy, St. Thomas turns to the fundamental reason. Such forceful baptism would do violence to natural justice. For the natural order of things demands that, before a child comes to the age of discretion, he should be cared and provided for by his parents, in matters of both body and soul; natural law enjoins, says St. Thomas, that in all matters a child be in his parents' charge and care. It would therefore be against natural justice if he were taken away from his parents, or any serious arrangement were made in his regard against their wishes; it is for them alone to make decisions on his behalf. It would therefore be a precisely similar violation of natural justice to baptize a child against his parents' wishes as to baptize an adult against his. However, once a child has attained years of discretion, he is entitled to care for himself, in matters of both divine and natural law. He may then be led to the Faith by persuasion, though never by force, and may embrace it if he chooses, even if his parents are unwilling.

Throughout the treatment of the five objections, St. Thomas insists that the rights of the parents are rights in strict justice, rights in the most full-blooded sense possible. The spirit of his replies is, "Fiat iustitia, ruat coelum"; no purpose, however exalted, can justify a breach of natural justice.

The first objection is an *a-fortiori* argument based on what is called the "Pauline privilege". The bond of marriage is stronger than the right of parental authority over children, the objector argues; for the latter can be set aside by man, as when a son is emancipated, but the former cannot, as Christ's words enjoin[1]; but the marriage bond is dissolved on account of unbelief, as St. Paul[2] and the canons[3] provide; *a fortiori*, then, the right of parental authority is forfeit on account of unbelief; so unbelievers' children may be baptized against the parents' wishes. St. Thomas replies that in the case of the marriage bond, each party, as an adult, has the use of reason and freewill, and so each can embrace the Faith without the other's consent. But this is precisely the point he has made about children: before they come to the age of discretion the natural order of things provides that decisions in their regard are to be made by their parents. The parallel with marriage holds, however, after they reach adulthood.

[1] He quotes Matt. 19.6, "What God has joined, let no man put asunder."

[2] He quotes 1 Cor. 7.15, "If the unbelieving partner is for separating, let them separate; in such a case, the brother or the sister is under no compulsion."

[3] He quotes from the contemporary canon law, caus. 28,9,1: "If the party who is an unbeliever refuses to live on without blaspheming the Creator, the other party is not bound to cohabitation."

The second objection is again an argument *a fortiori*. It is sinful to fail to help a man whose mortal life is in danger: it will be much more sinful, then, to fail to help a person whose eternal life is in danger; but the children of unbelievers are in this very peril if they are left with their parents and reared in unbelief; therefore, says the objector, they should be taken away from their parents, baptized, and brought up in the Christian faith. But St. Thomas' reply is intransigent, and provides us with a principle central to our whole project. You cannot run counter to civil law to rescue a man from temporal death; for example, it is not lawful to procure by force the escape of a criminal justly condemned. Similarly, you must not break the natural moral law, which places a child in his father's charge, even to rescue him from the danger of eternal death. This is fidelity to principle indeed, and provides us with a principle of cardinal importance. Natural rights are inviolable, however exalted be the good that they hinder.

The third objection argues that the children of a bondsman are bondsmen too; but Jews are the bondsmen of kings and princes; so their children are also; consequently, says the objector, kings and princes are entitled to do what they will with Jewish children, and no injustice is done in baptizing them against their parents' wishes. St. Thomas' reply stands on the same principle: Civil bondage, he says, is bounded by and subject to the natural moral law. This laconic reply seems an eloquent vindication indeed of the rights of all men against the exaggerated claims of princes.

The fourth objection is couched in terms of a Cartesian-like dualism that is un-Aristotelian, and very un-Thomist indeed. A man's soul comes from God, and his body from his father, says the objector; he therefore belongs to God much more than to his father; it cannot be unjust, then, to take a child from his unbelieving parents and consecrate him to God by baptism. In his reply, of course, St. Thomas makes no concession to such dualism. Man, who is an undivided unity, is directed to God by reason. Before this direction can be given by his own reason, the natural law provides that it be done by the reason of his parents. They alone, St. Thomas insists, have the right to make decisions in his regard concerning the things of God.

The final objection is another argument *a fortiori*. Baptism does far more for a person's salvation than preaching does; yet the danger that results from neglect of preaching is imputed to the man who neglected to preach; *a fortiori* then, says the objector, if Jewish children are in danger of being lost through neglect of their baptism, the guilt lies with those who could have baptized them and did not, namely, the

Christian political power. This objection simply gives St. Thomas another opportunity to make his point. The blame for neglected preaching is imputed only to those who were commissioned and charged with the responsibility for preaching; but the charge and responsibility of seeing that children receive the sacrament belongs to nobody but their parents. No blame attaches to the civil authority for not having these children baptized, for the parents alone have the right to make decisions in their children's regard concerning the things of God.

2. FREEDOM FROM "COMPULSION TO BELIEVE"

St. Thomas devotes an article to the question, "Should unbelievers be forced to accept the Faith?"[1] He answers with a distinction. Unbelievers who have never been Catholics must never be compelled to embrace the Faith; but heretics and apostates are to be forced, physically if need be, to fulfil the promise they once made. At this stage we shall follow only the discussion on the first limb of the distinction, namely, that part of the article which forbids the use of compulsion on those who have never been Catholics.

The argument is very simple. The act of faith is essentially a free act; without an interior, free choice of the will there is no valid act of faith at all. It is therefore not lawful to use compulsion

[1] Q. 10. art. 8.

in any way to force Jews or pagans to accept the Christian faith. With regard to making the initial act of faith, St. Thomas accepts St. Augustine's principle, "A person can do other things against his will; but belief is possible only in one who is willing."[1] A man may sign a contract, join a firing-squad, pronounce an oath of allegiance, without any interior consent; but unwilling belief is an impossibility. The only valid act of faith is that which proceeds from a free, interior choice. Therefore, no-one is to be compelled to believe. At the same time, a stipulation is added: the faithful are entitled to defend themselves against unbelievers who assault the Faith by blasphemous utterances or even open persecution. This may be exercised by strong believers on behalf of their weaker brethren persecuted in other lands, so that war against unbelievers is lawful to prevent their persecuting the Faith. But the point is repeated: in the event of a Christian victory, should unbelievers be taken prisoner, they must be left complete freedom in the matter of embracing the Faith.

It will be noticed that St. Thomas seems to advocate freedom for Jews and pagans, not out of respect for their rights in justice, but out of concern for the healthy fervour of the Faith. He certainly thinks it wrong to force anyone to join

[1] Quoted in the third objection from Augustine's *Tract. XXVI in Ioann.*

the Church; but under what moral description is it wrong? His answer to this question was quite clear in the case of baptizing children against their parents' wishes: that would be a breach of the virtue of justice, because it would be to violate the parents' right. I hope to establish the same claim with regard to compulsion of the adult himself, namely, that a person has a right to immunity from compulsion in religious matters, and that an offence against this right is an act of injustice. But St. Thomas makes no such suggestion here. His reason seems to be that a forced statement and external acceptance of Christianity would not be genuine, and so would enfeeble the robust religious health of the Christian body, and also, presumably, involve the sacrilege of an insincere and unworthy reception of the sacraments.

This is not very reassuring. Whenever we meet an argument, "Do not do X, for fear that Y may follow," we are afraid that X *will* be done if it can be shown in a given case that Y will not follow, or that something worse than Y will. This is always a disturbing element in any form of ethical consequentialism. However, such fears are groundless here. In the treatise on baptism St. Thomas once more studies the question of baptizing the children of unbelievers against their parents' wishes. He concludes:

> It would be an offence against natural justice if such children were baptized against their

parents' wishes; just as it would be if an adult were baptized against his.[1]

Although it is a pity that St. Thomas does not give his reasons for the latter half of this contention, the categorical statement is reassuring. Forcing a person to join the Church against his wishes is an act of injustice, and St. Thomas believes that an act of injustice cannot be justified for any good purpose in the world.

However, St. Thomas sees no connection between this question and that of the duty not to act against conscience. It is not only the principle, but the very example used in his earlier article which seems to demand attention.

> Belief in Christ is, of itself, something good, and necessary for salvation. But if one's reason presented it as something evil, one's will would be doing wrong in adopting it.[2]

This would seem an obvious argument to invoke. He holds that to profess faith in Christ against one's personal conviction is sinful. On his own showing, then, the question, "Should unbelievers be forced to accept the Faith?" is equivalent to the question, "Should a person be forced to commit sin?" This would seem to be a more immediate reason for holding that Jews and pagans must never be compelled to embrace Christianity.

[1] *ST*, 3,68,10.
[2] *ST*, 1–2,19,5.

2. ST. THOMAS AS THE OPPONENT OF FREEDOM

WE now turn to the aspects of the case which I, for one, find disappointing. Bluntly, there are two rights which St. Thomas would deny: the right of heretics to life, and the right of all unbelievers to practise their own form of worship. Admittedly, these two summary phrases must be qualified, and we shall find that his opinions are not so harsh as this brief statement sounds. None the less, even when St. Thomas advocates mercy for the unbeliever, it *is* mercy, and not justice, which prompts any suggestion of lenient treatment; he does not think that the refusal of these liberties infringes the *rights* of the people concerned.

1. THE RIGHT TO LIFE

It has already been seen that St. Thomas was unreservedly opposed to the use of pressure on people who have never belonged to the Church. However, his views are quite different with regard to those who were once Catholics, and have lapsed into heresy or apostasy. Those views are set out in three articles which, despite some slight overlapping, had best be taken up in turn.

It is important to be clear about St. Thomas' terminology. He applies the word "heretic" only to those who once were Catholics but now, though still claiming to be Christians, have rejected one or more Catholic doctrine and hence have ceased to belong to the Church.[1] In the following pages, therefore, the words that St. Thomas speaks of "heretics" have no application to the born Anglican or Protestant of the present day. The same is true of his use of the term "apostates"; this refers only to those who once were Catholics and have now totally renounced Christianity. The apostate differs from the heretic in that he rejects the whole Christian revelation, whereas the heretic still retains the name "Christian" and accepts many Catholic doctrines, while rejecting one or more of them; but both "apostate" and "heretic" are used solely of people who once were Catholics.

First we return to the article entitled, "Should Unbelievers be Forced to Accept the Faith?"[2]

---

[1] The modern popes normally follow the usage of St. Thomas. They speak of other Christian groups as "dissident" Churches or communities; the word "heretic" has acquired an offensive tang, and is accordingly not used of our separated brethren. Cf. C. H. Davis, "Faith and Dissident Christians", *Clergy Review*, April 1959, pp. 215–6. He quotes G. Baum, *That They May Be One*, London, 1958, pp. 40–64.

[2] Q. 10, art. 8.

As we have seen, St. Thomas makes a distinction. On the one hand there are Jews and pagans, who have never belonged to the Church; these, he says, may never, in any circumstances, be forced to accept the Faith. On the other hand there are heretics and apostates, who once accepted the Faith and have now renounced it, in whole or in part; what of them? The answer is brief and blunt:

> There are other unbelievers who at one time accepted the Faith, and professed[1] it; they must be compelled, even by physical force, to carry out what they promised and to hold what they once accepted.

It is important first to be clear that the overwhelming majority of people outside the Church today do not fall under his argument; they did not once hold and profess the Catholic faith, nor promise it their loyalty. They belong to the first class discussed in this article, namely, those who have never belonged to the Catholic Church. St. Thomas' principles therefore forbid a "Catholic state" to exercise compulsion on born

[1] The text actually has the present tense, *profitentur*, without question in the five editions I have consulted. This is puzzling; the apostate is precisely the person who does not in any way profess the Christian faith. I have therefore rendered the word in the past tense, as the sense of the passage seems to demand. The English Dominicans do the same in their translation.

Protestants with a view to forcing them to adopt the State religion. "People who have never accepted the Faith must not, on any account, be forced to embrace it."

However, although this is the conclusion reached from applying St. Thomas' principles to our own present situation, there remains his less practical but most unpleasant attitude to the Catholic who renounces his Faith. We are inclined, at first, to say that the statement is made without any argument being offered; but then we notice that the reason for the attitude is implicit in the phrase "to carry out what they promised"; it is wrong to force an uncommitted person to accept the Faith, but, he argues, it is right to compel a person to honour a promise he has freely made. This is made much more explicit in the reply to an objection based on Augustine's principle, "A man can do other things against his will; belief is possible only in one who is willing"; the objector remarks that external force cannot touch the will, and concludes that no-one must be compelled in matters of belief. St. Thomas replies by drawing a parallel to the obligation to keep a vow. A person must be completely free before he can take a vow, and no obligation to take it can exist; but once a vow is taken, there is a strict obligation to keep it. Exactly the same is true of the Faith, St. Thomas argues: there must be perfect freedom before a valid act of faith can be made; but once it is made, freedom is ended. We might strengthen his case by suggesting the parallel of a contract. There must be real freedom for a person to make a valid contract; but once it is made he is no longer free, and may be forced to fulfil the undertaking he has made. It is lawful, he concludes, to enforce the promise a man once made in embracing the Catholic faith.

Such an argument, however, is hard to reconcile with two other principles which St. Thomas defends elsewhere. He holds that a person cannot promise to do something sinful, or rather, that should he so promise, he is under no obligation to keep his word; for instance, he condemns King Herod, not merely for having made his rash vow to Salome, but also for enjoining its fulfilment.[1] But he also holds that it is always sinful to act against one's conscience, and specifically that it is sinful to believe in Christ if one thinks this to be wrong.[2] On his own principles, then, the appeal to the propriety of enforcing the baptismal promise seems to fail. Of course, given the conditions of his day, St. Thomas did not consider it likely that a person could cease to see the truth; our own experience is, unhappily, very different; but in any event,

---

[1] *Commentary on St. Matthew's Gospel*, cap. 14, at "Propter iusiurandum".

[2] *ST*, 1–2,19,5.

we are not here concerned with factual questions of how likely it is that such a thing should occur or how frequently it actually happens. Most theologians since the Vatican Council consider it certain that nobody can lose the Faith without grave personal fault; but that does not bear on our present point. Our concern is with a question of principle; what of the person who, in fact (whatever antecedent fault is to blame), has come to think that the Catholic Faith is untrue? His misfortune is that he does not believe; to act as if he did would therefore (on St. Thomas' own principle) be wrong. *Here and now* his position is the same as that of the person who never believed; in his case, therefore, as in that of any other unbeliever, the question, "Should unbelievers be forced to accept the Faith?" would seem to be equivalent to the question, "Should a person be forced to commit sin?"

The parallel with a vow is sometimes invoked to deal with another difficulty; how can there be an appeal to a *secular* court to enforce *religious* obedience, or to give judgement against a heretic on a point of religious dispute? Will this not imply that the civil authority has jurisdiction in purely spiritual questions? It has been suggested that St. Thomas could argue that it is perfectly proper for the Church to approach the secular courts against the heretic on the grounds of breach of contract. This does not involve crediting the secular judge with competence *in spiritualibus*, for the judge is not to make an authoritative pronouncement on a disputed point of religious doctrine; the Church's representative is to be present in court simply as one party to a contract which the other party has failed to fulfil. For this he seeks redress.

But the redress he seeks is of a special kind. He does not seek damages; he seeks the coercive power of the court to enforce "specific performance", namely, of the contract of membership. Of course, there are some matters in which a court quite properly enforces specific performance. But where "specific performance" involves a free, interior act of the will, this is not so. Thus, in a case of breach of promise of marriage, the court may quite properly find that damages are due to the offended party; but it will not force the defendant to marry the plaintiff willy-nilly, for the marriage contract must, of its nature, be completely free. How much more is this true of the act of faith, which of its nature is uniquely interior, personal, private and free. Once again, the plea that the "defendant" used to have the Faith, or lost it through his own fault, is beside the point. The fact is that, here and now, he does not believe; and belief cannot be enforced or produced by Act of Parliament or the decision of a court. "That faith without which 'it is impossible to please God' must be the perfectly free 'homage of intellect and will'."[1]

One of the objections considered by St. Thomas in this article is based on Christ's parable of the tares.[2] The answer to it is of some historical importance, since it shows St. Augustine's reversal of opinion. The objection recalls that, when the householder was told that an enemy had sown tares among his wheat, he directed that the tares should not be rooted up for fear that the wheat be torn out with them, from which St. John Chrysostom concluded that heretics found among the faithful should not be put to death. One might add that Chrysostom's argument seems to be based not on the possible injustice to the heretics, but on the danger to the faithful; "If you kill heretics, you will certainly kill a number of the faithful at the same time", he says.

Now, against this interpretation one may remark that the immediate intent of Christ's parable was not a prescription, but simply a prophecy. He privately explained the parable as meaning that wicked men will be permitted to exist among the good until the end of time; only then will they be rooted out.[3] However,

[1] Pope Pius XII, Encyclical *Mystici Corporis*, London, Catholic Truth Society, 1956, p. 62.
[2] Matt. 13.24–30.
[3] *vv.* 36–43.

St. Thomas remarks that some people applied the parable as an argument for excommunicating heretics, and others as an argument for putting them to death; as, for example, did St. Augustine. At first, Augustine had believed that no-one should be forced into union with Christ, but (we read with dismay) he was led by experience to change his mind, and invoked the parable of the tares to justify his later, harsher view; you do not root up the tares if by doing so you endanger the wheat, but you do if no such danger exists. St. Thomas accepts St. Augustine's conclusion in its verbatim ugliness:

> When the heretic's guilt is so well known, and people find it so loathsome, that he has no-one to defend him—or at any rate, not such as could lead to schism—there must be no leniency in his punishment.

This is distressing indeed, and the first time of reading it is not a proud moment for those of us who love St. Thomas. There is nothing surprising in his standing by his scale of values and insisting that spiritual goods must be sought at the expense of temporal, and the good of the many preferred to the good of the few. He was fond of quoting Aristotle, "The good of the whole people is more godly than the good of one man"; how much more does this hold (he is urging) when it is a case of comparing the supernatural good of the many with the natural good (namely, the life) of one man. But our reaction is not against the scale of values which St. Thomas is holding, but against the suggestion of an unfeeling and ungallant calculation of numbers and prospects in which the heretic with powerful and influential supporters will escape, but the poor dissenter who has no friends to stand by him suffers the full rigour of the law. At least it is a comfort to find a little further on that the two saints are by no means as insensitive as this reply might suggest; St. Thomas again quotes St. Augustine:

When the Catholic Church saves the many by losing the few, the grief in her motherly heart is assuaged by the deliverance of great peoples.

However, our substantial disappointment is not with the tone of the first reply, but with St. Thomas' failure to study any connection with his own earlier principles concerning the obligation to follow one's conscience. If the heretic believes in good faith and sound conscience here and now (even though because of some earlier fault of his own) that the Catholic Faith is untrue, then while that unhappy position continues he is obliged not to return to it. How can it be lawful to force him to do something which he is obliged not to do?

A different argument is put forward in the second article devoted to the issue of the unbeliever's right to life. It occurs in the question devoted specifically to heretics, and is entitled, "Should Heretics Be Given Toleration?"[1] It quickly becomes clear that the sense of the question is, Should they be allowed to go on living?

From the point of view of their crime, says St. Thomas, they should not; not only should they be banished from the Church by excommunication; they should be banished from the world by death. The life of the soul is much more precious than temporal life; but it is a capital offence to counterfeit money, which serves temporal life; *a fortiori*, then, to corrupt faith, which is the life of the soul; therefore heretics are quite rightly put to death. However, from the point of view of the Church, there must be mercy; she is bound to seek the conversion of those who stray, and must obey St. Paul's injunction[2] to give a first and a second warning. But if the heretic proves obstinate, and there seems to be no hope of his conversion, St. Thomas concludes, she must provide for the safety of the many, banish him from membership by excommunication, and see that the

[1] Q. 11, art. 3.
[2] Tit. 3.10.

secular tribunals banish him from the world by death.

There are two points of fact that may first be noted. One is the relatively small point that, in most civilized countries, forgery is no longer a capital offence, and, in general, punishments are milder than those imposed by medieval courts. Would St. Thomas yield to the trend towards leniency? On his own argument, he would have to insist that the heretic be not at large as long as he was actively corrupting the faith of others; perhaps detention during the Queen's pleasure would be a modern equivalent. A more significant point of fact is to insist that, in the present day, members of other Churches, or of none, are not heretics in St. Thomas' sense. His harsh words do not apply to the born Anglican, Protestant, Jew or agnostic.

Next, the argument raises difficulties on the score of Church-State relationships. The secular judge is competent to judge matters concerning the currency of the realm; but whence comes his jurisdiction to judge cases involving religious doctrine? If it derives from the State, then the State would seem to be enjoying competence in the purely doctrinal field; if it derives from the Church, then civil authority would appear to be originating from the Church. However, the argument can be dealt with independently of this problem, which is beyond the scope of the present book.

Our central objection relies on St. Thomas' own principle: No end, however exalted, can justify a violation of natural justice. One wants to invoke this at each stage of his argument. He has argued that the good of the many must be preferred to the good of the few; but this is not true when the good of the many can be procured only by unjust means, by a violation of natural justice. He has argued that the preservation of the integrity of the Faith must be pursued even more strenuously than the preservation of the purity of the national currency; this is true, but it does not justify the employment of injustice, the violation of a right. In the light of this very principle of the inviolability of natural justice, St. Thomas twice rejected arguments on behalf of the spiritual needs of unbelievers' children; certainly, charitable concern for their eternal welfare would demand baptism for the children, were it not for the fact that baptism against the wishes of their parents would violate natural justice. We have already seen how uncompromising was St. Thomas with regard to the inviolability of justice:

St. Paul says, "God remains true to his word; he cannot disown himself." But if God set aside the order of his justice he would be disowning himself. And so, God is not able to dispense a person from a right relationship to him, nor from subordination to the order of justice which he has declared, even when it is a case of justice as between man and man.[1]

So far, of course, the right to freedom of conscience in religious matters has not been established in this essay; that will be the aim of the final chapter. But even before it has been argued, one certainly feels that there is an onus of proof which St. Thomas has made no attempt to discharge. If there is so strict a right in regard to one's *children* that not even their eternal loss can justify its violation, how much more may we expect a right in regard to one's *conscience*? There is a far more intimate relationship between a man and his conscience than between a man and his children. This lack of proof becomes all the more curious when one recalls St. Thomas' own principle that it is never lawful to act against one's conscience, even though the matter at issue be that of believing in Christ. I suggest then that, since this presumption is not rebutted, St. Thomas has failed to make his case. Once again he disappoints our hopes of seeing a study of the connection between the present problem and his own earlier principles concerning the obligation to follow one's conscience.

[1] *ST*, 1–2,100,8 ad 2.

One other article bears on the unbeliever's right to life. It is entitled, "Should Penitent Heretics be Received Back by the Church?" The gist of St. Thomas' reply is that the Church must always receive back the repentant heretic and restore to him all the spiritual goods at her disposal; but this does not apply to the temporal goods she controls.

His argument is based on the duty of charity, which the Church is bound to extend to all men, friends, foes, and even persecutors. Now, charity demands that we desire and seek our neighbour's good, which is twofold: spiritual and temporal. The spiritual good, the salvation of the soul, is the essential object of charity, and this we must desire for all men unconditionally. It follows, then, that whenever a heretic seeks to be admitted back into the Church, he must always be received, no matter how often he has fallen.

The secondary object of charity is our neighbour's temporal good—life, property, good name, dignities; charity binds us to seek this for him only in so far as it conduces to the eternal salvation of himself and of others. If, therefore, any temporal good of one person is an obstacle to the salvation of many, charity does not bind us to seek it for him: rather we should want him to be without it, for supernatural good is to be preferred to any natural good, and the good of many to the good of one. But, says St. Thomas,

if we always save the life and goods of the
penitent heretic, this will be an obstacle to many
other people's salvation; partly because, should
he lapse again, he may infect others with his
heresy, partly because if he goes scot-free, others
will lapse into heresy without fear of punishment. St. Thomas recommends, therefore, that,
on the first occasion that a person repents of his
heresy, he not only be welcomed back to the
spiritual riches of the Church, but also his life
be spared and his dignities restored. But should
he lapse again, this seems to suggest inconstancy
about the Faith itself; the Church, then, should
always accept his repentance and give him every
spiritual aid and comfort, but do nothing to save
him from sentence of death.

Let us not retrace the arguments submitted
already against the general line of this article,
but merely criticize specifically what is new in
it. All that St. Thomas says about charity is clear
and telling, and we may agree with him quite
literally that it is not charity that demands the
heretic's freedom from death; it is justice. It is
quite true that the virtue of charity takes into
account a hierarchy of goods and a hierarchy of
persons, and that a duty in regard to a lower
member of these hierarchies yields to the demand of a higher. This is mostly reduced to the
rule of thumb, "Serious personal suffering or
loss excuses one from an obligation of charity",

and, of course, danger to spiritual welfare is the greatest of all "personal sufferings". But no such principle holds with regard to the obligations created by the virtue of justice. As has been urged more than once already, St. Thomas himself holds that no objective, however exalted, can sanction a breach of justice. Yet such a breach occurs, I hope to show, when force is used to come between a man and his religious convictions, more so even than when it is used to come between a man and his child's religious affiliation, which St. Thomas himself brands as a breach of justice.

2. THE RIGHT TO WORSHIP

St. Thomas devotes one whole article to the question, "Should There Be Toleration for the Religious Rites of Unbelievers?"[1] This clearly does not refer to the faithful who fall away into heresy or apostasy; where the Church has the power to do so, he thinks, she should have them put to death. This article concerns those who have never had the Faith at all, and who must not in any circumstances, St. Thomas holds, be compelled by force to embrace the Faith. Given that they must not be constrained to practise the Christian religion, may they be permitted to practise their own?

[1] Q. 10, art. 11.

His answer begins with the proposition that God, in his government of the universe, permits some evils which he could prevent, for fear that, in removing them, greater goods might be lost or worse evils might follow. In this the wise human ruler will follow God: it is on this principle (says St. Thomas) that Augustine would tolerate the existence of prostitutes. Hence, although unbelievers sin by their worship, tolerance is permissible if it leads to some great good or prevents some great evil. Consequently, Jews may be permitted to practise their rites, since these prefigured the Christian faith, to which they now bear witness; but the rites of other unbelievers have neither truth nor utility to commend them, and should not be tolerated except to prevent some greater evil; such an evil might be scandal, civil unrest, or an obstacle to the salvation of those who, if left in peace, might gradually be converted to the Faith. For these reasons, the argument concludes, the Church has sometimes extended toleration to pagan and heretical worship when unbelievers were in large numbers.

There are four lines of criticism that suggest themselves against this argument. The first is to demur at the whole tone of the article. Freedom of worship is not an evil to be grudgingly tolerated, let alone put on a par with the licensing of prostitutes; it is a right to be respected in natural justice. The second is to ask, Whose good is to be the criterion for determining which rites are to be permitted, which not? Apparently only the faithful's; then what body is charged with procuring the common good of the others, for which the natural law must provide? Unbelievers are creditors and debtors of the natural law as much as any Christian. The third is to challenge the statement that unbelievers sin by their rites, and to argue that this is at odds with St. Thomas' earlier position on the authority of conscience. The fourth follows naturally on the third. It is to consider the evil whose prevention would follow from granting toleration. However, not all of these points will be taken up here. The first is the concern of our final chapter, when we seek to reconstruct the argument for the right to freedom of conscience. The second could be discussed only in a study of Church-State relationships. Here we shall pursue only the third and fourth of these criticisms.

First then, what of the statement that unbelievers sin by their rites? This is the most explicit assertion of an assumption that has often been felt as latent in St. Thomas' writings on unbelief. At first sight it appears to be at odds with his own earlier statement, "In the case of people who have never heard of the Faith, unbelief is a matter, not so much of guilt, as of punishment."[1] But the two statements are not strictly incompatible; the earlier article was treating merely of the unbelievers' ignorance, the absence of all knowledge of and assent to the Christian revelation; the present one is claiming that in following their own religious belief and practising its rites, they sin. This is a hard saying.

Let us imagine a distant people living, and practising religious rites, before God's revelation to Abraham. Presuming that their rites involve no immorality, they certainly commit no sin. At what moment do their rites become sinful? Presumably, when God reveals his will that he be worshipped in a certain way, and issues a command to that effect. But St. Thomas himself has anticipated that line of argument; his own terminology is that "negative unbelievers" are those who have heard nothing of God's message or commands; and his own principle is, "No-one is bound by a law save by one means only: knowledge of that law." There seems to be no gainsaying this.

It is disputable whether we may even say that such people commit "material sin", that is, fail objectively to keep the law. If it were natural law that was in question, this might well be argued. But when it is positive law, which cannot in any way be known without access to the legislator's wishes, this is not easy to maintain.

[1] Q. 10, art. 1.

Whatever of this, we insist on the crucial point: not only does St. Thomas offer no proof for his statement that unbelievers sin in celebrating their own rites; as a universal statement, it is contradicted by his own principles concerning ignorance and responsibility. At such points one is keenly aware of the different historical contexts in which these questions are studied by St. Thomas and ourselves. One is conscious of the confident concealed premiss never far below the surface of St. Thomas' argument: "To see, yet not to accept the Church, surely argues bad faith." Our own times are very different, and we should feel that such generalizations were simply not true to the facts. But in any event, the point of the present criticism is not with matters of fact, but with a question of principle: given that a person *is* in good faith, how can he sin by practising the rites which his conscience enjoins?

The other criticism of this, Article Eleven, concerns the evil whose prevention would follow from granting toleration. Once more no attempt is made to connect this issue with the principles established in the *Prima Secundae* with regard to moral authority of conscience. Here in the *Secunda Secundae* it is held that the rites of unbelievers may be tolerated if this will help to prevent some evil, such as civil unrest or scandal. Civil unrest is indeed an evil; but to be untrue

to one's conscience is a greater evil, for it is evil
in the moral order. If, therefore, the danger of
civil unrest justifies religious toleration, how
much more so will the danger of forcing people
to be untrue to their conscience, when it enjoins
on them a particular religious observance? With
the mention of scandal, our hopes are raised; for
in the writings of the scholastics, "scandal" has
not its modern English meaning of malicious
gossip, or outrage and indignation; for them, it
occurs when one person occasions another's sin
"by injunction, inducement or example".[1] What
then of an injunction or law which occasions a
person to sin by not following his conscience?
But once again we are disappointed; St. Thomas
does not advert even to the existence of the
problem.

It could be misleading to conclude this
chapter without recalling its limited objective:
namely, to consider St. Thomas' views on the
freedoms to which unbelievers are entitled, in
the light of his analysis of the concept of conscience and his views on its moral authority.
Any general appraisal of his writings on religious freedom is beyond the scope of the
present work. Such an appraisal cannot be made
simply by a study of his text, but would have to
be undertaken in conjunction with a thorough

[1] ST, 2-2,43,1c.

understanding of the social context in which he wrote. Two elements in this context may be mentioned.

First, one would need to understand well the distinction between two essentially different types of political régime; to use the terminology of Monsignor Journet, and of Jacques Maritain, the consecrational régime under which St. Thomas lived and wrote; and the secular régime with which alone we are familiar. In the course of his study of this distinction, Journet warns us against passing a hasty judgement on St. Thomas' text without considering its context:

> St. Thomas' reasoning proceeds under the double supposition (1) of a state consecrationally Christian, and (2) the legitimacy of the death penalty for crimes against the State. To neglect these suppositions is to condemn oneself to understand nothing of his thought, and to see no more in his argumentation, for all its clarity, than a subject for scandal.[1]

Second, one would need to remember how different was his experience of contact with "unbelievers" from our own, and how different the reactions it engendered and the assumptions it fostered. Given the luminous, monolithic reality of the Church in his day, St. Thomas

[2] C. Journet, *The Church of the Word Incarnate*, London, Sheed and Ward, 1955, p. 285. The study of the nature and implications of a régime of "consecrational" Christendom is found in ch. 4, pp. 214–324.

tended to think that anyone who saw it and did not embrace it must be either fool or knave. We who have come to be so sensitive to others' consciences, and to individual differences of intelligence, and the refracting medium of centuries of history often laden with bitter or shameful memories, tend to say, Hardly ever a knave, sometimes a fool, most often a person of good will inculpably unable to see the reality. For our contemporaries, the climate of opinion is unfavourable to belief; for St. Thomas it was so favourable that he apparently finds it difficult to conceive unbelief except as ill-will.

A general appraisal of St. Thomas' account, then, is not to be lightly undertaken; but with regard to our own specific problem, a sense of dissatisfaction remains. The principles concerning the authority of conscience in the *Prima Secundae* raise expectations that they will be applied in those parts of the *Secunda Secundae* that deal with the freedoms due to religious dissenters; but the application is never made. The reconciling of the two trends of thought would seem to be a major problem; yet St. Thomas nowhere shows himself aware of the need for such reconciliation; it does not arise even in the objections which he urges against his conclusion. Indeed, in the eighteen articles devoted to the topic of unbelief, the very word "conscience" does not once occur.

PART IV

PART IV

A RECONSTRUCTION
OF THE ARGUMENT:
THE RIGHT TO FREEDOM
OF CONSCIENCE

MANY political philosophers outside the Catholic Church argue for the right to religious freedom from a premiss of doctrinal indifferentism; "One religion is as good as another," they say, "so people of all faiths should have like freedom before the law." Although (as I believe) their premiss is mistaken, their logic is perfectly sound. But then they sometimes advert to the fact that Catholics reject doctrinal indifferentism, and so presume that we will also deny the right to religious freedom. In this their logic is not so good; they seem to be committing the old logical fallacy "denying the antecedent": "If p, then q" does not license the inference, "But not p, therefore not q." On the other hand, there have been Catholics who have felt scruples about endorsing such rights as those set forth in the United Nations Universal Declaration of Human Rights, which claims for everyone, without distinction of any kind, religious or otherwise,[1] the right to freedom of

[1] Art. 2.

thought, conscience and religion in teaching, practice, worship and observance.[1] They have feared that a person who holds for the right to freedom of conscience might find himself committed to holding for religious indifferentism. Behind such fears there seems to lie the obverse logical fallacy of "affirming the consequent": "If *p*, then *q*" does not license the inference, "But *q*, therefore *p*." If a person is a Mahommedan, he believes in one God; but not all monotheists are Mahommedans.

The United Nations Declaration is not concerned to elaborate any theoretical justification for the rights it sets forth, and many Catholic philosophers and theologians have sought a basis for them in sound principle. Such efforts have been stimulated by the accession of Pope John XXIII, and the memory of his address to UNESCO in 1951. During his time as Apostolic Nuncio in France, Archbishop Roncalli was appointed by the Holy See as its first permanent observer to that specialized agency of the United Nations Organization. Speaking to the Sixth General Conference of UNESCO, he praised the way that it pursued "the ends of justice, liberty and peace for all peoples of the earth, without distinction of race, language and religion"; and, repeating that phrase, he insisted that the different religious spirit and values of different

[1] Art. 18.

peoples should be respected.[1] The trend and the spirit of such words is naturally most heartening to those Catholic writers who would find a theoretical justification for the rights proclaimed in the United Nations Declaration.

The present chapter seeks to do so. It argues that every adult has a strict right to religious freedom, and that the State is guilty of injustice if it interferes with a person's following his conscience in matters of religious choice, profession and worship. It holds that the right is satisfactorily recognized and protected in such documents as the constitutions of the Commonwealth of Australia, the Republic of Éire, and the United States of America.

In presenting such an argument, can one claim to be putting forward "the Catholic view"? To answer that question, one must first draw a distinction between negative and positive religious freedom: the right to negative freedom guarantees that one shall not be forced to accept someone else's religion; the right to positive freedom means that one is entitled to practise one's own.

The demand for negative freedom, as a matter of strict justice, is held by all Catholic writers, in common with St. Thomas: "It would be an offence against natural justice if children were

[1] Quoted by A. Giovanetti, *We Have A Pope*, London, Geoffrey Chapman, 1959, p. 91.

baptized against their parents' wishes; just as it would be if an adult were baptized against his."[1] Furthermore, this is not merely the unanimous opinion of Catholic philosophers and theologians, but is the official teaching of the Church. Pope Pius XII wrote:

> If it ever were to happen that, contrary to the unvarying teaching of this Apostolic See, a person was compelled against his will to embrace the Catholic Faith, we could not, for the sake of our office and our conscience, withhold our censure.[2]

With regard to positive freedom, however, different Catholics hold different views. There is one school of thought which holds that every adult has a strict right to religious freedom, and that is the view espoused in this chapter. Other Catholic writers, however, believe that the governments of "Catholic states" are not bound, at least as a matter of principle and strict justice, to extend the right to freedom of conscience to members of other religious denominations, or of none. Each school is naturally concerned to argue that its opinion is more closely in harmony with the authoritative documents of the Church; but in the absence of any definitive statement de-

[1] *ST*, 3,68,10.
[2] Encyclical *Mystici Corporis*, 29 June 1943, *AAS*, 35 (1943), p. 243.

voted to the question *ex professo*, neither can claim that its opinion is "the Catholic view".

There is another reason for saying that the case presented in this chapter cannot claim to be "*the* Catholic view". The only argument put forward here is that based on the moral authority of conscience; but Catholics who hold that all men are entitled to religious freedom often consider that the principal argument for their position is that which is based on the freedom required to make a valid act of faith. For instance, Pope Pius XII argued as follows for the conclusion just quoted:

We do indeed desire that the whole mystical Body pray to God unceasingly for the speediest possible entry into the one fold of Jesus Christ of all those who are astray; but we declare that it is absolutely necessary for this to be done freely and willingly, for no-one believes unless he is willing. If therefore a person, not believing, were forced to enter a church, approach the altar, and receive the sacraments, he would certainly not become a true believer in Christ, for that faith without which "it is impossible to please God" must be the perfectly free homage of intellect and will. If therefore it ever were to happen that, contrary to the unvarying teaching of this Apostolic See, a person was compelled against his will to embrace the Catholic Faith, we could not, for the sake of our office and of our conscience, withhold our censure.[1]

This then, is often presented as the main basis of the right to religious freedom: freedom is required for a valid act of faith, and justice demands that every man enjoy the freedom needed to make such an act. At the same time most writers who share the view defended in this chapter agree that the argument based on conscience is a sound one, if secondary; they will naturally refer to other words of Pope Pius XII which apply—at the very least—to negative freedom:

> In the case of people who are not Catholics, the Church applies the principle taken from the Code of Canon Law, *No-one shall be forced to embrace the Catholic Faith against his will.* She considers that their convictions are a reason, although not always the principal reason, for tolerance.[2]

And again:

> Out of respect for those who are in good conscience—mistaken indeed, but invincibly so—and of a different opinion, the Church

[1] *Mystici Corporis, AAS,* 35 (1943), p. 243.
[2] Allocution *Vous avez voulu,* to historians, 7 Sept. 1955, *AAS,* 37 (1955), p. 679.

has felt herself prompted to act, and has acted, along the lines of tolerance.[1]

It is only the argument based on conscience which is the concern of this essay, and this final chapter sets out to state one version of it.

[1] Allocution *Ci Riesce*, to jurists, 6 Dec. 1953, *AAS*, 35 (1953), p. 801.

1. THE ARGUMENT

ONE premiss of the argument is provided by the conclusion of our second chapter: there is an absolute duty never to act against conscience; if a person has reached a certain judgement of conscience in good faith, he has an obligation to follow it. Can we argue from the principle that one has a *duty* to follow conscience, to the principle that one has a *right* to do so?

Let us be clear about what we are doing. It is obvious enough that there is one sort of logical connection between some rights and some duties. Thus, if A has a right to x, then B has a duty to A in regard to x; as Reid says:

> [Right and duty] have the same relation which credit has to debt. As all credit supposes an equivalent debt, so all right supposes a corresponding duty. There can be no credit in one party without an equivalent debt in another party; and there can be no right in one party, without a correspondent duty in another party.[1]

If A has a right to be paid for his professional services, then B has a duty to pay A when he

[1] *Works*, vol. 2, p. 643.

receives them. St. Thomas has already provided an important example: since parents have the right to care for their children's spiritual welfare, others have a duty not to interfere in the matter. But this is not our task. We are not concerned to argue:

"A has a right" *entails* "B has a corresponding duty"

but to argue:

"A has a certain duty" *entails* "A has a corresponding right."

Certainly, to the extent that we succeed in proving that A has a *right* to follow his conscience, to that same extent others have the duty to respect it; and indeed a duty in justice. But this is just the point. Can we prove that "the absolute *duty* of a man not to act against his conscience" gives rise in him to "a strict *right* not to be compelled to act against conscience"; and further, can we prove that the *duty* to follow one's conscience gives rise to a *right* to follow it?

There is a troublesome point of terminology which calls for attention before the Thomist account of "right" is examined. The Latin word *jus* is ambiguous, corresponding sometimes to the English *right* and sometimes to the English *law*; and the ambiguity is reproduced in the

French *droit*, the Italian *diritto*, and the German *Recht*. The English word "right", when used as a noun, has no such ambivalence; we see the shadow of the other senses of *jus* in such words as "jurist" and "jurisprudence"; but the noun "right" never leaves us wondering whether it means a law, or a claim in justice. This is a distinct advantage for English-speaking political philosophers, but calls for some care when reading Latin or Continental writings.

Hobbes felt something of the difficulty:

> Though they that spake of this subject used to confound Jus and Lex, right and law, yet they ought to be distinguished; because Right consisteth in the liberty to do, or to forebeare; whereas Law determineth, and bindeth to one of them; so that law and right differ as much as obligation and liberty.[1]

But it was Austin who recognized it most explicitly, and his note on it is so clear (and perhaps entertaining) as to make it worth quoting in full:

> In the Latin, Italian, French and German the name which signifies "right" as meaning "faculty" (i.e. the noun), also signifies "law": "jus", "diritto", "droit" or "recht", denoting indifferently either of the two objects. Accord-

[1] *Leviathan*, Everyman ed., London, Dent, 1953, p. 66.

ingly, the "recht" which signifies "law", and the "recht" which signifies "right" as meaning "faculty", are confounded by German writers on the philosophy or *rationale* of law, and even by German expositors of particular systems of jurisprudence. Not perceiving that the two names are names respectively for two disparate objects, they make of the two objects, or make of the two names, one "recht". Which one "recht", as forming a *genus* or kind, they divide into two *species* or two sorts: namely, the "recht" equivalent to "law", and the "recht" equivalent to "right" as meaning "faculty". And since the strongest and wariest minds are often ensnared by ambiguous words, their confusion of those disparate objects is a venial error. Some, however, of these German writers are guilty of a grave offence against good sense and taste. They thicken the mess which that confusion produces, with a misapplication of terms borrowed from the Kantian philosophy. They divide "recht" as forming the *genus* or kind, into "recht" in the *subjective* sense: denoting by the former of those unapposite phrases, "law"; and denoting by the latter, "right" as meaning "faculty".

The confusion of "law" and "right", our own writers avoid: for the two disparate objects which the terms respectively signify, are commonly denoted in our own language by palpably distinct marks.[1]

Other distinctions that can be made concerning the terms *jus* and "right" have been noted by Bentham[2] and Melden[3]; but the only one which is important for the present discussion is that between *jus*, meaning "right", and *jus*, meaning "law".

1. THE THOMIST ACCOUNT OF "RIGHT"

It is the modern Thomist account of a right, rather than that of St. Thomas himself, which we shall find most helpful. He was inclined to speak in such terms as, "Justice demands that A have x," rather than, "A has a right to x"; for example, the discussion to which we referred as, "The rights of parents concerning their children's religion", was discussed by him in such terms as, "Natural justice demands that a parent have charge of his child in all important matters."

He devotes a question to the topic of *jus* at the beginning of his treatise on Justice.[4] He

[1] John Austin, *The Province of Jurisprudence Determined etc.*, London, Weidenfeld and Nicolson, 1954, pp. 287–8, in the footnote.

[2] *Principles of Morals and Legislation*, ed. W. Harrison, Oxford, Blackwell, 1960, p. 424, n. 2.

[3] *Rights and Right Conduct*, p. 1.

[4] *ST*, 2,2, q. 57.

opens the treatise with this discussion, because
he holds that *jus* is the object of the virtue of
justice, and devotes the first article to that
proposition; but the article does not help our
own inquiry very much. It contrasts justice with
other virtues on one point, namely, that we
assess what is right and good where other virtues
are concerned by reference solely to the agent,
i.e., whether or not a given act contributes to his
own perfection; but where justice is concerned,
by reference to the agent in comparison with
something besides himself. Indeed, says St.
Thomas, this is how we assess an action as just
or not; provided it attains the just object, the
action is called just, regardless of the agent's
motive; whereas we do not style an act as
charitable or chaste or pious unless both the
object of the act and the motive of the agent are
sound. If a man gives alms to the poor in order
to escape taxation, or to curry favour with
electors, we do not say that his action is
charitable; but we do say that a man's action is
just when he pays a debt, even though it be
only in order to escape legal action or loss of
employment. The answer to the first of the
objections in this article remarks that there are
several senses of the word *jus*. The primary one,
St. Thomas says, is "the just thing itself", but
other senses include the art of discerning the
jus, and the office of administering it. In English

these are secondary usages of "law" rather than "right"; which sense of *jus* is intended? One hopes to be given the answer when St. Thomas distinguishes between *jus* and *lex* in his reply to the second objection. First, he says, comes *jus*, which exists in the mind; then the *lex* expresses it in writing. This is not what we had expected; and subsequent articles confuse us further. They seek to separate *jus naturale*, *jus positivum* and *jus gentium*, and show very clearly the different origin of each of these; but at several points we are uncertain whether *jus* is referring to the right of an individual, or to law.

The modern Thomist treatise on justice is, in general, largely indebted to that of St. Thomas, which is, as a whole, a helpful study of the virtue and its implications; but, specifically with regard to the account and terminology of rights, it has strong echoes of Locke, and the American and French Revolutionaries who drew on him in the century that followed. Pope Leo XIII and his successors seem frequently to have made use of Locke's terminology, and in papal writings we often find discussions couched in the concrete and personalistic language of "rights" which St. Thomas might rather have pursued in the more abstract terms of "justice"; and many Thomists have followed the popes in this preference.

As a matter of emphasis, to be sure, one may

contrast the approaches of Locke and the writers of the eighteenth-century "Declarations" on the one hand, and Thomists on the other. For the former, the starting-point was the individual person, and natural rights were conceived as "simple and indisputable truths", "truths that are self-evident". These were, so to say, the axioms from which other principles were to be deduced after the fashion of theorems. It is a little odd that the rights claimed by the revolutionaries as self-evident were not always the same. The Virginians claimed as "self-evident and inalienable" the rights to life, liberty and the pursuit of happiness. The French, in the Déclaration of 1789, named as natural and imprescriptible rights "La liberté, la propriété, la sureté et la résistance à l'oppression." The constitution of 1793 listed "L'Égalité, la liberté, la sureté, la propriété." All of these, as Ritchie remarks,[1] owe a great deal to Locke, who recognized the natural rights of life, liberty and estate. Despite these differences in detail, the starting-point in all these theories was the individual person, and a number of self-evident rights inherent in him. In the Thomist approach there is a difference, at least in emphasis. The starting-point is, rather, an objective order of

[1] D. G. Ritchie, *Natural Rights*, London, Allen and Unwin, 1924, ch. 1, especially p. 6.

ends and values, in which the subjective element of "right" takes rise in a relationship created by this order.

However, this contrast should not be exaggerated. The Thomist also sees this objective order as rooted in something ultimately individual: the end of the individual person, the value of the individual destiny, which may never be subordinated to any other end or destiny. It is really here that the Thomist finds the seat of all right and all created law: in the personal destiny of the individual man. St. Thomas' philosophy of human nature, confirmed and enriched by his theology, led him to conclude that each man has a unique, sovereign value and a unique, sovereign destiny or end which cannot be subordinated to any other purpose on earth. He would have been delighted, one feels, with Kant's principle, "Always treat men as ends, never simply as means." This is the controlling principle, the absolute to which all lesser proposals must be referred, and in whose light they must be judged. "Finis specificat media": the demands of natural justice will be embodied in an objective order of ends and values whose members will be determined, and whose hierarchy settled, by reference to the sovereign value and the ultimate end inherent in the individual human person.

Given the refinements introduced by Lockians and the modern Popes, then, contemporary Thomists are able to give a more thorough analysis of a right than did St. Thomas. They often distinguish between subjective right, the claim residing in the person, and objective right, the total resultant situation which includes his claim and the duties of others in regard to it. This is not a terminology that fits naturally into English, and indeed writers in English still seem to have some advantage on this topic, and have no problems about the relationship between *jus*-meaning-"right" and *jus*-meaning-"law". Even now, writers in Continental languages give different accounts of this distinction. For instance, Genicot sees the two uses of *jus* as simply a loose sense and a strict sense[1]; whereas Aertnys gives "*jus*-meaning-'right' " as the primary sense, from which "*jus*-meaning-'law' " is derived "by way of causality, since law stands in a causal relationship to subjective right."[2] But in English we feel no temptation to use the word "right" for the justice-situation, as for instance does Père Delos in his admirable study:

> A right is a certain arrangement of men and things between themselves. It establishes an

[1] *Institutiones Theologiae Moralis*, vol. 1, p. 388.
[2] J. Aertnys and C. Damen, *Theologia Moralis*, Turin. Marietti, 1932, p. 433.

objective order between individuals, so adjusting their mutual relations as to create a justice situation between them.[1]

It is interesting to notice here that the word "justice" appears in the definition; this, therefore, cannot be the primary sense of the word "right"; the primary sense is the subjective right, which in fact is the only sense the noun has in English. Genicot's definition is typical of any contemporary Thomist:

Subjective-right is defined as a person's moral power to have or to do something for his own benefit, no-one being reasonably able to object.[2]

The words "for his own benefit" are decisive as between the strict sense of the word "right", and its looser senses. Thus, in a sense, the Sovereign has rights over his subjects; but this is a loose sense, for he holds these rights for the good of his subjects, not of himself. But the employer acquires strict rights over his employee, for these are intended for his own benefit; as are the employee's rights against him. But given that we are concerned with right in the strict sense, what does the definition reveal?

[1] J. T. Delos, writing in the "Renseignements techniques" in the volume *La Justice* of the French translation of the *Summa* already quoted, p. 230.
[2] Vol. 1, p. 388.

It is clear that, properly speaking, a right exists only between several persons, and its effect is to establish a certain relationship between them. But it is not an immediate relationship. Rather, it is a relationship between these persons resulting from the different relationships they bear to some object. Let us call the object to be had or done O, and the person who has some grounds for a claim upon it, the subject, S. The fact of his having a ground for a claim on O is not sufficient for the existence of a right; the presence of a third term, P, is essential for a right in the full sense. O is the nexus of a relation between S and P; the reason for their relationship lies in the fact that O has connections with both S and P: different connections with each, creating between them a new relationship, whose nature and extent it determines.

The first connection is between O and S. Here there is the relationship of "belonging", so that the correct use or situation of O is that it redound to the profit of S, "for his benefit". But this is not sufficient to establish a "right". To complete the concept, there must be another person, who has such a relationship with O that there also arises a relationship between him and S. Faced with the object that belongs to S, new duties arise for P. A moral duty now exists for him towards S precisely with regard to O, and in accordance with the standard set by O. He is now in duty bound to respect the right of S and should he fail in this duty is guilty of "injustice". Such an analysis leads Delos to the following definition of objective right:

> A right is a complex whole comprising two persons and an object, the persons being joined by a relation of which the object is the term which both unites them and determines the character of the relationship. In other words, a right exists when an object is the term of two different relations which it controls and renders correlative.[1]

A recent discussion in circles very far from the Thomist tradition sounds almost like an echo of this account; three of those involved are English-speaking philosophers from, as it happens, three different continents. Father Delos' analysis of a right is very like Professor Baier's analysis of an obligation.[2] Baier distinguishes three logical dimensions in an obligation: the partner, who is mentioned in answer to the question, "*To whom* is A under an obligation?"; the ground, mentioned in answer to this question, "*On account of what* is A under an obligation to B?"; and the content, mentioned in answer to the question, "*What* does A's obligation to B

[1] p. 232.
[2] Baier, *The Moral Point of View*, Ithaca, Cornell University Press, ch. 9.

consist in?" He argues from this that moral obligations can exist only as relationships between
at least two people, and that immoral conduct
consists solely in what is harmful to others.[1] Professor Hart has criticized such views on the
grounds that it is a mistake to use the words
"duty" and "obligation" for all cases where there
are moral reasons for saying that an action ought
to be done or not done; "duty", "obligation",
"right", and "ought", he says, come from different segments of morality.[2] In making a distinction between obligation and duty, two of his
criteria remind us very much of Delos' account
of a right: obligations, says Hart, are owed to
special persons (who have rights); they do not
arise out of the character of the actions which are
obligatory, but out of the relationship existing
between the parties. Professor Frankena has criticized Hart for asserting that *rights* and *obligations* belong to one area of morality, and *"ought"*
and *duties* to a separate one; and for holding
that rights entail obligations but do not entail
duties.[3] He feels that it sounds odd to say that

[1] A view attributed to Aristotle by St. Thomas.
(*ST*, 1–2,18,9 ad 2.)
[2] H. L. A. Hart, "Are There Any Natural Rights?"
Philosophical Review, April 1955, p. 179. It was not
Baier's particular version that Hart was contesting, but
that of those who spoke as Baier subsequently wrote.
[3] W. K. Frankena, "Natural and Inalienable Rights",
Philosophical Review, April 1955, pp. 214–5.

one has a duty to relieve suffering, but no obligation to do so.

At all events, the Thomist account concludes that, in order to establish the existence of a right, i.e., of a requirement of justice, in a given situation, we must show two things: first, that the subject in question has some ground for a claim on the object at issue; second, that he has not merely this ground, but the moral power to urge this as against some other person or persons.

One common way in which this arises is by contract. An example is a contract for professional services. The object in question is, say, legal representation; the subject is the client, who agrees to pay for the services of the barrister in his case, and from this there arises a right to these services, which gives rise to a strict duty on the part of the lawyer to render them to him. In this case, nobody is under obligation resulting from this contract except the two parties who enter it.

The marriage contract creates wider obligations. The object in question here is the act of sexual intercourse. The parties to the contract are the husband and the wife, so that now neither may deny the other the right to intercourse when it is reasonably demanded. But other people are also affected by this contract, and obliged to respect it. A third party cannot now have intercourse with one of the married people without being guilty of injustice to the other. If a man performs this act with a single woman he is guilty of unchastity, but—if she be willing—not of injustice. But to perform it with a married woman is to be guilty also of injustice, a violation of the exclusive right of the woman's husband.

2. APPLICATION TO FREEDOM OF CONSCIENCE

What are the terms or the elements of the right we are seeking to establish in this chapter?

The subject is any sane adult human being. On the one hand, lunatics and infants do not have moral responsibilities, and are not in question. On the other hand, our discussion is obviously not confined to the Christian faithful, but is meant to embrace every person having the actual use of reason.

The object is an action, the following of one's conscience. This involves immunity from external force compelling one to act against one's conscience, immunity from external force denying one the ability to follow one's conscience, and the "full possession of privilege", the faculty and freedom to perform these actions which conscience enjoins, without let or hindrance. Here we shall not range over the whole field that this might imply, but shall consider specifically the freedom of one's conscience with regard to religious choice, profession and worship.

The "third party" against whom the right is claimed is civil authority, the State. This applies to the State whether it acts of its own inspiration and for its own purposes, or at the behest of some other body or group.

It is clear, then, what are the two elements we must establish to vindicate the right involved in the relationship of these three terms. First, we must show that a man has some ground for a strict claim to freedom of conscience as described. Second, we must show that he can validly urge this claim against the State.

(i) THE GROUND

The ground on which it is here suggested that the claim to freedom of conscience is based is the absolute duty never to act against conscience. Clearly, we have to deal here with a right which has a very different origin from the rights we have mentioned earlier. The lawyer's client and the married person derive their rights from a contract. But essential human rights derive from the natural order itself, and belong to what St. Thomas calls "natural justice"; the more intimately a given "object" (in the broad sense) is connected with the integrity of the human personality, the more stringently is it protected by natural justice. When it comes to a question of life, St. Thomas holds that not even the safety of many innocent people can abrogate the right to life of the innocent man. Here the S is the innocent man, O the object is his life, and O bears such a relationship to S that it creates so stringent a duty both in the State and in others that nothing can justify its direct violation. In this sense the right is absolute. It is not unlimited, for the State may jeopardize life, i.e., permit danger to life as a foreseen but unintended by-product, but only when comparable goods are at stake; one may think of the example of compulsory military service in time of war. We have seen that another right was credited with an even tighter protection: confronted with the proposal that Christian princes should use their great powers to baptize forcibly unbelievers' children, St. Thomas allowed that the end was a noble one—the supernatural life of the child—but could find no way of attaining it without violating natural justice. How are we to account for the emergence of these rights which are not created by contract?

It might seem tempting to picture an argument such as the following: Each man has a supreme, individual destiny, beatitude after death; this is sovereign and ultimate, and cannot be subordinated to any other purpose on earth. From this a number of natural rights would be deduced: in so far as a certain object is necessary for a man to attain this end, to that extent he has an inalienable right to it. From this, in turn, the duties of other people in his regard would be deduced; in so far as a man has an inalienable right to a given good, to that extent others have a strict consequential duty in justice to respect it. Such a rigorously deductive system might seem promising enough; and it would be an easy matter to conclude to the right to freedom of conscience on lines such as the following: It has been established that it is never morally lawful to act against one's conscience; given this, and given that a person cannot win his ultimate reward unless he is substantially faithful in meeting his moral obligations, it would be concluded that he has a natural right to follow his conscience, from which, in turn, it would follow that the State had a strict duty to respect his freedom to do so.

But this is not the Thomist approach. We may well remember the warning we proposed to ourselves concerning the precepts of the natural law.[1] "Good must be done and evil avoided", we found, is not the primary principle in the sense that from it all others are deduced; we compared it rather with the principle of non-contradiction in the speculative order. One does not deduce all the truths of metaphysics from the principle of non-contradiction; it is, rather, the formal prin-

[1] Cf. *supra*, pp. 50–55.

ciple which controls and governs all our syllogizing. So in the practical order, the principle
"Good must be done and evil avoided" is not
one from which we deduce all the precepts of the
natural law; it is the formal principle which
governs all "practical" syllogisms. We found that
there was not one single principle from which all
the others can be deduced; rather, one has to
begin from the inclinations in which the primary
precepts are expressed, and from them, several as
they are, the others, primary and secondary, are
to be derived.

One might expect a similar warning to hold
here, since in Thomist theory the demands of
natural justice are part of the whole kaleido-
scopic complex of natural law. It is true that
St. Thomas' is a teleological ethic, but this does
not imply a "monist" teleology. It is not that
St. Thomas names a single, simple, ultimate end
from which we rigorously deduce a hierarchy of
proximate ends, from which in turn we rigorously deduce, with increasing particularity, the
means needed for attaining each of them. The
ultimate end of beatitude after death does not
act as a kind of universal major premiss from
which all subordinate means, rights and duties
are necessarily derived by discursive ratiocination. Perhaps such a theory would promise certainty (if it could be successfully launched), but
as an account of the good life it would be bleak

and austere indeed, and is certainly not the Thomist concept.

In fact, the starting-point of Thomist theory is not an end conceived as a major premiss, but the human person with its multiple and bewildering complex of goods and potentialities. It is the human person, rather than his end, who is sovereign and ultimate; or, to be more accurate, it is indeed the end of the individual person, but this is not to be narrowly conceived as the attainment of happiness after death, but the far more complex end of the total harmonious fulfilment of the potentialities of the individual person. The statement of the case in terms of a monist teleology would, incidentally, render unintelligible two claims on which we have seen St. Thomas to be uncompromising. First, if happiness after death were the sole and sufficient determinant of conduct, the single premiss of a deductive system, how could St. Thomas support the right of the unbelieving parents against the Christian prince's intention to baptize their child? Given his theological datum, that only baptism can gain an infant admission to beatitude, all lesser rights would be overridden and subordinate. Second, how could he forbid the taking of one innocent life to save many? If eternal life were the only end which cannot be subordinated to others, it would follow that mortal life can be subordinated to other ends.

Such claims, however, are naturally expected in an ethic of "pluralist teleology". In such an ethic, natural-law theory is not a system of rigorous deduction from a single premiss, but rather like a spectroscope discovering the multiple constituents of a complex whole. It will find that there are some goods which cannot be taken from the human person without damaging the integrity of the whole; yet it will often leave to the individual person the arrangement of these goods, the choice between them when they clash, the particular subordination of one to another. Herein is to be sought the resolution of a tension that has often been felt in the course of this essay. On the one hand, it can be seen why St. Thomas insists that no end, however exalted, can sanction a breach of natural justice; for this is equivalent to saying that it is the person who is sovereign and ultimate in the dispositions of natural justice; thus, compulsory mutilation in the interests of medical research, or of the genetic advantage of the community, will be forbidden. On the other hand, the subordination of one human good to another *within the one person* will lie within his own choice. For instance, the voluntarily accepted amputation of a diseased organ in the interests of the health of the whole body will be lawful, since it is chosen as a means to another good by the person in whom natural justice deposits the power of choosing between the many goods that make up the ensemble of his "end".

The Aristotelian antecedents of this theory are obvious. Wherever change in fulfilment is possible, existence belongs first to a subject of potentialities and powers, which is what Aristotle and Aquinas mean by "substance". This is quite a different concept from Locke's complete, static substance, to which qualities or accidents are added like icing to a cake or pins to a cushion. When a person performs an action—say, of speaking or thinking or writing a book—he is exercising an ability, a power, that was really there all along. When a person acquires knowledge or skill or virtue, he is not then a person *plus* knowledge, skill or virtue; he *becomes* a knowledgeable, skilful or virtuous person. The ability to become these things was there all along. The subject of these abilities is thus conceived as a principle of development or fulfilment, and the fulfilment as its end or immanent purpose. In the case of man this immanent purpose is complex indeed, and ideally will consist in the harmonious fulfilment of a great wealth of potentialities, that is, the achievement in due proportion of a multiplicity of goods.[1] Such a theory will obviously call for some skill in choosing between different goods, and in recognizing

[1] Cf. D. J. B. Hawkins, *Nature as the Ethical Norm*, Blackfriars, 1951, p. 10.

the means needed for their pursuit. It does not deny the end of final beatitude after death; indeed St. Thomas sees the perfecting of potentialities in the present life as equipping one for the maximum enjoyment of the vision of God, which his theology promises. Aristotle helps Aquinas to see beatitude, not merely as some "thing", extrinsic to the successful traveller, won by him and received: rather, the good moral life is the development of human powers for the maximum appreciation and enjoyment of the vision to come. Admission to bliss is at once the ultimate end of human striving, the reward merited by fidelity to moral duty, and the fulfilment of all the human capacities for joy.

This makes our task easy just when it might have seemed to become too difficult. Obviously there will be room for dispute about many goods that contribute to the fulfilment of the human person. Should the virtue of patriotism be subordinated to the family virtues in wartime, or vice versa? Must the enjoyment of sex in marriage be subordinated to the power of procreation, or not? Must the good which is freedom of speech be subordinated to the good which comes from public peace and order? Many such questions call for the nicest discernment and judgement, within the hierarchy of human goods, before the demands of natural justice are settled. No detailed settlement will ever command unanimous agreement; one is reminded of Mr. Hare's approach to the major premiss of moral syllogizing mentioned earlier in this essay.

But in our own investigation the good in question is indisputably supreme: the sovereign end of the human person. One of the conditions for attaining this is substantial fidelity to moral duty; and this, as our earlier inquiries found, consists in following one's conscience. Therefore the possibility of so following conscience is a strict demand of natural justice. Where there is question of goods that contribute helpfully, but not indispensably, to the integral perfection of the human person, he has a conditional claim upon them; it is conditional, namely, on its being compatible with the comparable goods of other people; it can be subordinated to the common good. But where there is question of goods that contribute as necessary conditions to the sovereign end of the individual person, the claim is unconditional; natural justice forbids its subordination to any other end. St. Thomas instances our mortal life as being such a good, and therefore as being so protected by natural justice; but moral integrity is a greater good even than mortal life; therefore it creates a still stronger claim to that which is needed for its attainment, namely, the freedom to be faithful to the dictates of conscience.

And yet, some would object, is this to be consistent? It was claimed above that the ultimate end of man is not merely some extrinsic "thing" handed to a man at the end of his life, in the nature of a prize for a good performance; it is also the harmonious intrinsic development of his personal potentialities, brought to bear upon the subject of beatitude when he is admitted to its presence and sight. Now, surely this opens up a line of thought contrary to our claim. It is notorious that a man often "does not know what is best for him". The doctor will often recommend a line of action quite contrary to our own inclinations; but it will normally be his prescription that contributes best to the perfection of our person. So with the prosecution of the higher goods of the moral order. The expert, perhaps State-appointed and State-empowered, may well know best (it is objected) what contributes to our higher perfection. We may not like it, but it will be in our best interests that he decide for us what is best for our own good, and see that we do what contributes most effectively to the fulfilment of our moral potentialities.

St. Thomas has provided us with the answer to this in the arguments we previously studied. A man's moral fulfilment and stature is measured above all by the performance of his will; the will, in its turn, is assessed according to its conformity with its own proper object. But the proper object of the will is not the good as it exists objectively, or as it is known to some moral genius with a skill and an insight superior to one's own: it is the good as apprehended and presented to a man by the judgement of his own reason. Of course, one of the elements of the decision which one's reason ultimately makes will be the guidance of authoritative and skilled moralists whose standing we accept; but it has to be the individual's judgement of conscience that this *is* an authority which we may safely accept. As Mr. Hare says, other people cannot make decisions of principle for us unless we have first decided to take their advice or obey their orders. This seems to be the meaning of Newman's famous but otherwise puzzling paragraph:

> Certainly, if I am obliged to bring religion into after-dinner toasts (which indeed does not seem quite the thing), I shall drink—to the Pope, if you please;—still, to Conscience first, and to the Pope afterwards.[1]

The extent to which the individual is faithful to his own sincere appraisal of what is good and right for him, in the total situation that confronts him, is the measure of his performance.

One cannot but feel again the disappointment occasioned by some of the views of St. Thomas

[1] *Difficulties of Anglicans*, London, Longmans Green, 1910, vol. 2, p. 261.

studied in the third part of this book. It was from him that we derived the principles concerning the authority of conscience; it was from him that we derived the principle that the goods that stand highest in the scale of ends and values are protected by natural justice; regrettably, he never seems to have seen the bearing of the one upon the other. At all events, it is by making the connection between these principles that the *ground* of the right to freedom of conscience is argued.

(ii) THE THIRD PARTY

Our analysis of the concept of a right revealed that, in order to vindicate a right in the strict sense, two things must be established: first, that the person in question has some *ground* for a claim on the object in question; second, that there exists a *third party* against whom he may validly urge the claim. A second point, then, remains to be established before we have successfully proved the right to freedom of conscience: can we show that one may validly urge that claim *against the State*? To be sure, this might well be regarded as a simple corollary of the demand made by natural justice. But a ground is not yet a right. Could it be that there is some special feature of civil authority that renders it immune from or superior to the individual citizen's claim to freedom of conscience?

The acceptance or rebuttal of this possibility will turn on our view of the purpose of the State: does the individual exist for the State, or the State for the individual? If man exists for the State, then all his *prima-facie* rights will be tempered by its high reasons and policies. It would be aimless to urge the sovereignty of the individual moral conscience against, say, Hegel's transcendent "Ethical State". In an early essay, *The Scientific Treatment of Natural Law*, he had claimed that natural-law theory is nothing but an *ex-post-facto* generalization of existing institutions, which could never offer a complete morality. "The absolute ethical totality is nothing but 'ein volk'—a people or nation."[1] In his more mature *Philosophy of Right* we find Hegel elaborating this view, and holding that the national state is the highest embodiment of ethical life, and that its "right" supersedes every other. Machiavelli's blunt contrasting of the demands of morals and politics led to the convenient empirical doctrine of the *raison d'état*, which explained, if it did not excuse, the encroachments of political necessity on the field of accepted morality. But if, as Hegel holds, history is the necessary evolution of the Absolute towards perfect self-consciousness, and the State is conceived as the embodiment of ethical life,

[1] Quoted by A. P. d'Entrèves, *Natural Law*, London, Hutchinson, 1951, p. 72.

the exigencies of the *raison d'état* appear in a very different light. There is no longer simply an empirical statement of how things are; as a matter of principle, this is how things should be.

> The welfare of the State has claims to recognition totally different from those of the welfare of the individual. The ethical substance, the State, has its determinate being, i.e., its right,[1] directly embodied in something existent, something not abstract but concrete, and the principle of its conduct and behaviour can only be this concrete existent, and not one of the many universal thoughts supposed to be moral commands.[2]

Such a rejection of the view that natural justice imposes universal and inviolable obligations is the logical and proper corollary of the view that the individual person exists for the sake and service of the State.

St. Thomas' view is very different from this: man was not made for the State, but the State for man. This may be too blunt a statement, for he does not conceive the community merely as a means to an end, and speaks of the different societies as having their own immanent ends and

---

[1] Here is an instance of the ambiguity of the German *Recht*. Should this be translated "right" or "law"?

[2] C. W. F. Hegel, *The Philosophy of Right*, trans. T. M. Knox, Oxford, 1949, p. 215.

their own values. Nevertheless, it is in the needs of the individual that these originate. A sketch has already been given of the Thomist theory of the sovereign and ultimate value of the individual, and his natural right to whatever things are needed for his full development as a human person. In particular, there is his need for social and political life. Life in an ordered society is necessary for the fulfilment of man's potentialities and inclinations. This explains at once the origin, the purpose, and the limitations, of the State in Thomist theory.

The origin of the State is to be sought in man's natural tendency to live in society, and his recognition of his need for it if he is to enjoy the fullest possible development of his material, sexual, cultural and moral capacities. But St. Thomas argues that social life, to be orderly, demands social authority as a natural and necessary requirement if many different persons are to live in tranquillity and order.[1] This directive power, or political authority, belongs to the State.

The purpose of the State is accordingly conceived by St. Thomas as helping man to attain his end. We have already rejected the narrow conception of the end of man as salvation after death, and seen it as a much richer and more subtle complex of goods to be pursued and values

[1] *ST*, 1,96,4.

to be ordered and prosecuted. This order of
goods and values is partly expressed in, and protected by, what St. Thomas calls natural justice.
It is in the light of this that we see both the
extent and the limits of State authority. To some
extent the powers of the State will be conferred
and limited by the choice of the citizens it is to
serve. The powers conferred on the Commonwealth Parliament in Section 51(i) of the Australian Constitution, differ from the powers
conferred on Congress in Section 8, a-r, of the
United States' Constitution, and these differences
are determined by the will of the people who
gave themselves and their rulers these constitutions. In this sense, political power is in the gift
of the citizens. But the possible differences are
not unlimited. One way of expressing the limitation is to say that no power can be validly conferred on a ruler which runs counter to natural
justice; this is the principle which we have
remarked so often as being held by St. Thomas.
But we show the fundamental reason for this
limitation more clearly if we point to the purpose assigned to political authority by natural
law. The purpose of the State is to help man to
attain his end, and from this purpose it derives
its powers. Therefore, anything done by the
State which thwarts the end of man, and makes
the attainment of that end difficult or impossible,
is, precisely to the extent of that difficulty or

impossibility, done *ultra vires*. The individual has the right to receive from the State whatever of the goods committed to her is necessary for the attainment of his end; therefore, in so far as the State renders the attainment of his end impossible, he suffers a violation of natural justice. But it has been found that substantial fidelity to moral duty is a condition of attaining one's end; and a person is untrue to moral duty if he acts against his conscience. This now leads us to the conclusion that, if the State forces a man to act against his conscience, it renders impossible the attainment of his end; it will therefore be violating natural justice and acting *ultra vires*.

It may be objected that this statement is an oversimplification. Life in society necessarily calls for frequent curtailment of private welfare in the interests of the common good, and quite often this curtailment will be determined and imposed by the State; and quite properly. "The good of the whole people is more godly than the good of one man." St. Thomas, it will be pointed out, was by no means an unequivocal supporter of private enterprise against public welfare. His argument in favour of capital punishment is a drastic illustration of this: just as it is lawful to amputate a diseased organ for the sake of the whole body's health, so it is lawful to strike away one corrupting member for the health of the body politic. This would certainly suggest

that the good of the individual must be subordinated to the common good. Indeed, St.
Thomas states this as a principle which seems
to be in direct contradiction to the view outlined above concerning the relations between
citizen and State.

> Every part is ordered towards the whole, as
> the incomplete towards the complete; and
> therefore every part exists for the sake of the
> whole . . . Now an individual person bears the
> same relation to the whole community that
> the part does to the whole. Therefore if any
> individual is dangerous to the community,
> and liable to corrupt it because of some sin,
> it is sound and praiseworthy to put him to
> death for the preservation of the common
> good.[1]

One's first reaction to such a line of argument
is that it proves too much. If each citizen is
merely part of the whole, then any dangerous or
infectious member should be struck away. Yet a
little later[2] St. Thomas holds that it is never
lawful, for any reason whatever, to put an innocent man to death. It is true that he had anticipated this charge of inconsistency by inserting
in the above passage the words "because of some
sin". But is this more than a verbal device? For

[1] *ST*, 2–2,64,2c.
[2] Art. 6.

if the individual stands to the community as the part to the whole, or as the member to the organism, there seems no difference in principle between killing the physically, mentally, or morally, defective. The real explanation seems to be that St. Thomas has in mind a datum of revelation: God, who has absolute power over life and death, delegates it to the State alone, and solely in the case of the criminal guilty of a grave offence against public order. Since the fact and the extent of any delegation depends entirely on the will of the delegator, it would seem impossible for the fact of God's delegating this mortal power to the State to be known except through his having revealed that fact. The appearance that the above passage presents of a proof from natural reason is therefore, perhaps, deceptive; it is a simile, and not a completely happy one, presenting a commonly accepted tenet of Christian (and pre-Christian, though revealed) religion.

The fact is that St. Thomas is not unequivocally clear on the relationship of citizen and community, of individual good and common good. Some of his most satisfactory remarks are blurred by qualifications of prudence, or perhaps of uncertainty. For instance, in studying the universal necessity of social and political life, he makes this very instructive distinction:

> The difference between the slave and the free man is this, that the free man exists for his own sake, whereas the slave's good is subordinated to someone else's.[1]

From this he concludes that the characteristic of the master-servant relation is that the master exercises his authority for his own profit and benefit, to serve his own ends. Not so where there is question of ruling free men:

> The feature of ruling a free man is this, that he is directed towards his own proper good.[2]

This is just the clarity we want; but the edge of it is then dulled a little when St. Thomas adds, "or towards the common good". No doubt enough has been said to show that, for him, the value of the individual person was sacred and the demands of natural justice inviolable, but one might have wished for sharper definition of their proper relationships with society and political authority.

Here, perhaps, modern Catholics have the advantage of him. He has provided them with the fundamental principles, and they have seen the elaboration of the theory and vocabulary of natural and inalienable rights conceived by Locke, developed by the American and French declarations, and refined by the popes. The

[1] *ST*, 1,96,4.
[2] *ST*, 1,96,4.

substance of modern Thomist theory does not differ from St. Thomas', but the expression is more felicitous, at once simpler and more sophisticated. For instance, Pope Pius XI wrote:

In the Creator's plan, society is a natural means which man can and must use to reach his destined end. Society exists for man and not man for society. It is life in a society which affords the opportunity for the development of all the individual and social gifts bestowed on human nature.[1]

Remarks of Pope Pius XII bear on the point even more directly:

The State must facilitate the attainment of the individual's physical, intellectual and moral perfection, and assist him to his supernatural end. Its purpose ... is to be defined according to the harmonious development and the natural perfection of man. It is for this perfection that society is designed by the Creator as a means.[2]

And again:

The divinely established natural order of beings and purposes constitutes each man an

[1] Encyclical *Divini Redemptoris*, 19 Mar. 1937, Australian Catholic Truth Society, pp. 15–16.
[2] Encyclical *Summi Pontificatus*, 20 Oct. 1939, Australian Catholic Truth Society, p. 15.

independent personality, the source and end of his own social life.[1]

The following words of Père Olivier may therefore serve as a summary of this second step in the argument:

The members of the State are human persons, and hence have an absolute value. It is the State's duty, therefore, to give its citizens the chance to achieve this destiny: society is made for man, not man for society. Society has no other end but the end of man himself; it must therefore help man in his pursuit of his end, it must help him achieve the real aim of his life ... This duty is imposed on the State by the transcendent character of its members: they are persons with a destiny going beyond that of temporal society, and with inalienable privileges that follow from this transcendent destiny.[2]

The first step, then, was to show that a person had grounds for a claim, in natural justice, to freedom of conscience. This second step sought to show that he could validly urge that claim against the State. It was felt that this might well be regarded as a simple corollary of the first step.

[1] *Christmas Allocution, 1944*, Australian Catholic Truth Society, p. 11.

[2] "The Rights of Conscience", in *Tolerance and the Catholic*, trans. G. Lamb, New York, Sheed and Ward. p. 158.

And yet the possibility was canvassed of there being some special feature of civil authority that renders it immune from this demand. However, far from finding that the State was empowered to override the freedom needed by the citizen to secure his personal end, the argument suggested that the State's purpose is to help man attain his end, from which purpose it derives its powers; consequently, in so far as the State prevents a man attaining his end, it acts beyond its powers. In brief, the citizen has the right to receive from the State whatever (lying within its power) is necessary to attain his end; therefore any action that prevents his doing so is an injustice; but if a man is to attain his end, he must follow his conscience; therefore where the State denies a man the freedom necessary to do so, it is acting *ultra vires* and against justice.

(iii) THE RELIGIOUS ASPECT

The rest of this chapter will be concerned with only one aspect of the possible applications of the right argued above: namely, the right to freedom of conscience in matters of religious choice, profession and worship. This demands both "negative freedom", i.e., that one must not be forced to accept someone else's religion, e.g., that of an official State Church; and "positive freedom", i.e., that one is entitled to freedom to practise one's own. Such freedoms are guaranteed in the written constitutions of many modern democracies, and it is interesting to note that, in the case of at least three such documents, the more recently they were drawn up, the more explicitly the rights of conscience in religious matters were formulated.

In the Constitution of the United States, the relevant passage occurs in the First Amendment, adopted in 1791:

> Congress shall make no law respecting an establishment of religion, or prohibiting the free exercise thereof...

The second phrase guarantees positive freedom of religion; the first phrase implies also a guarantee of negative freedom; conscience is not explicitly mentioned, but its rights are implicitly recognized, and protected. The Constitution of the Commonwealth of Australia was proclaimed in 1901, and the relevant passage occurs in Section 116:

> The Commonwealth shall not make any law concerning religion, or for imposing any religious observance, or for prohibiting the free exercise of any religion.

The first phrase, constitutional lawyers say, prevents the "establishing" of any one Church; the second and third phrases guarantee positive and negative religious freedom; conscience is not explicitly mentioned, but its rights are implicitly recognized and protected. The Constitution of "the people of Éire"[1] became law in 1937, and the relevant passages occur in the second section of Article 44:

(i) Freedom of conscience, and the free profession and practice of religion are, subject to public order and morality, guaranteed to every citizen.

(ii) The State guarantees not to endow any religion.

Conscience is mentioned explicitly; positive and negative religious freedom are both guaranteed; and no particular denomination can be erected as the official State Church. Each of these three statements, then, seems to be a satisfactory constitutional recognition of the rights for which this chapter has argued: freedom of conscience, both positive and negative, in matters of religious choice, profession and worship. Whether the argument further entails a conclusion concerning the propriety of an official State religion is beyond the scope of the present essay.[2]

[1] The Constitution nowhere explicitly designates Éire as a republic; it was in 1949 that Ireland formally became a fully independent Republic. Cf. S. Z. Ehler and J. B. Morrall, *Church and State through the Centuries*, London, Burns Oates, 1954, p. 593.

[2] There is an interesting contrast here between the United States and Great Britain. In Britain there is one denomination, the Anglican, privileged as the religion by law established, but care is taken to respect the consciences of people of other beliefs; and in particular there is respect for the rights of parents. In schools conducted by public authority, parents are free to

The United Nations Universal Declaration
of Human Rights deserves special mention.

---

choose what form of Christian, Jewish or other religious
education be given their child, or to choose that he be
given none. Furthermore, religious denominations are
free to conduct schools, and parents are free to choose
to send their child to one or other of them; and this
right of the parents is respected, not merely in the
weak sense that they are not forbidden to make such a
choice, but also in the strong sense that the school thus
chosen by the parents is entitled to a corresponding
share in public moneys raised for education, with no
privilege for schools of the State religion. In the United
States, on the other hand, there is no religion by law
established. In elementary and high schools conducted
by public authority, parents are refused the right to
choose or arrange religious education for their children.
Religious denominations are permitted to conduct
schools, and parents are free to choose to send their
child to one of them, in the weak sense that they are
not forbidden to do so; but not in the strong sense,
that all parents, whatever the school they choose, are
entitled to receive, or can nominate the school of their
choice to receive, a share in public moneys raised for
education; such moneys are reserved exclusively for
schools where no religion may be taught. This is frequently justified in terms of "the separation of Church
and State", an expression which does not occur in the
United States Constitution, but is often used to paraphrase the First Amendment. The slogan "No State Aid
for Church Schools", sometimes used in the United
States, as it is also in Australia, seems rather to miss the
point. It is not the rights of Churches or schools that
are at issue, so much as the rights of parents: their
right, namely, to make a free and equal choice between
existing types of school.

Maritain has remarked that it is an example of the fact that men can come to agree to a number of practical truths regarding their lives in common which are derived from extremely different, or even basically opposed, theoretical conceptions. He tells of a meeting of the French National Committee of UNESCO which was discussing the Rights of Man, at which someone expressed surprise that people of mutually antagonistic ideologies could yet agree on a proposed statement of the rights: "Yes," they replied, "we agree on these rights, *providing we are not asked why*."[1] At all events, the theoretical argument put forward in this chapter is embodied in practical terms in the Declaration. The second article lays down that everyone is entitled to all the rights and freedoms set forth in the Charter without distinction of any kind, religious or otherwise; and Article Eighteen spells out the particular aspect that concerns us:

Everyone has the right to freedom of thought, conscience and religion; this right includes freedom to change his religion or belief, and freedom, either alone or in community with others, and in public or in private, to manifest his religion or belief in teaching, practice, worship and observance.

[1] J. Maritain, *Man and the State*, London, Hollis and Carter, 1954, pp. 69–70.

When one thinks of the widely different, often mutually antagonistic, philosophies of the member nations, one feels that it was a remarkable achievement for those charged with drafting the Declaration to have produced a formula, at once acceptable to all the signatories, and so just and liberal in its provisions. St. Thomas insisted on the rights of parents concerning their children's religious initiation; the Declaration recognizes their rights in the choice of the type of schooling their children are to have: it is not denied that the State has rights in the matter of education, but, says Article Twenty-Six:

> Parents have a prior right to choose the kind of education that shall be given to their children.

And yet, this gives rise to an objection against the conclusions we have reached. Our argument was based on the claim that a person has a right to whatever he needs to attain his end. If there be conflict between this, and a lesser right of some other person or group, the latter's right must yield. Now, St. Thomas believes that baptism is strictly necessary for an infant to receive eternal life; perhaps an adult may achieve it "by some unconscious yearning and desire"; but for an infant baptism is indispensable. Suppose that the parent urges his right to choose that the child be not baptized; how can St. Thomas espouse this right of the parents against the highest of all needs of their child?

Such an argument presupposes a conception of natural justice which we have found to be incomplete. The end of man is not to be narrowly conceived as salvation after death, from which the precepts of natural justice are deduced as theorems from a single axiom; the truth is more complex, indeed, but much more worthy of the dignity of the human person. The end of man is to be sought in the full and harmonious development of his powers and capacities; and "natural justice" is an unchanging, though consequential, order of proximate ends, necessary means and hierarchically-graded values. Cardinal among these necessary means is that referred to in the principle that man attains his end through reason; indeed, more properly, the use of reason to achieve beatitude is an element in his end, rightly conceived. Now, the infant cannot use his reason personally; so the natural order directs that he exercise it vicariously, namely, through his parents. Were man's end narrowly conceived as salvation after death, then, the objection would hold: but the end of man, properly conceived, comprises many elements, and one of the most important of these is the development of reason and rational choice, in which, during childhood, one's parents are the vicars appointed by natural law. St. Thomas would seem to sympathize with such an approach; he writes:

> Man is directed to God through his reason, for it is by reason that he comes to know him. So it is that, before a child has the use of reason, the natural order directs him to God through the reason of his parents, to whose care nature commits him.[1]

Indeed, the argument can be turned against the objector. There is no relevant difference between the status of one who acts on another's behalf and one who acts on his own; but natural justice protects parents from State interference concerning their child's religion because they act in the matter on his behalf; therefore natural justice protects people from State interference concerning religion when they act on their own behalf. We were surprised that St. Thomas failed to see this inference in his treatise on the proper treatment of unbelievers; it is pleasant to recall that he drew it explicitly in his treatise on baptism, at least with regard to negative freedom:

> It would be a violation of natural justice if the children of unbelievers were baptized

[1] *ST*, 2–2,10,12, ad 4.

against their parents' wishes; just as it would be if an adult were baptized against his.[1]

One final point could be mentioned. The argument seems to demand more than that the State forbear from visiting religious dissenters with imprisonment, torture and death; social and economic pressure can often be sufficient to impel a man to act, and live, against his conscience. Indeed, the more drastic penalties may on occasion be so overwhelming as temporarily to swamp a person's responsibility, and exonerate him from personal guilt in momentarily renouncing his convictions; whereas prolonged social and economic pressures, although not having this result, may quite effectively induce the choice to live by a creed in which he does not sincerely believe, and hence to suffer personal spiritual ruin. It seems to follow, then, that justice demands that a person suffer no civil disabilities because of his conscientious religious profession; and this seems to be satisfactorily provided for in such constitutional guarantees as the following:

No religious test shall be required as a qualification for any office or public trust under the Commonwealth.[2]

[1] *ST*, 3,68,10.
[2] Constitution of the Commonwealth of Australia, from sec. 116.

The State shall not impose any disabilities or make any discrimination on the ground of religious profession, belief or status.[1]

... no religious test shall ever be required as a qualification to any office or public trust under the United States.[2]

[1] Constitution of Éire, art. 44, 2 (iii).
[2] Constitution of the United States, art. 6, c.

2. THE DIFFICULTIES

APART from St. Thomas' own arguments which have already been considered, there are two types of objection against the view espoused in this chapter which should be now examined; and finally there is the question of the limits of the argument.

1. THE DUTY TO PREVENT EVIL

The first objection is based on the premiss that one is obliged to prevent evil when it lies in one's power to do so; if another person is bent on doing wrong, but cannot do so without one's assistance, or acquiescence, or at least non-interference, then one is bound to prevent him; to allow him to act is to share his guilt. But, some people have proceeded to argue, pagan or heretical worship is wrong; therefore, if a person or group is bent on practising such false worship, or preaching false doctrines, the government which can prevent him is obliged to do so.

In some matters, of course, the line of the argument is familiar enough. Most governments feel it their duty to prevent murder, theft, slander, and so on; nor do democratic liberties necessarily extend freedom to people who are intent on and capable of destroying democracy. But does such reasoning also apply in religious matters? For people who believe that one religion is as good as another, or that objective religious truths cannot be discovered with any certainty, the argument has no application. As a Catholic I regret their holding such views; but at least it is a grateful thing that, in communities where such views are common, there is respect for the rights of conscience. This is true even where the prevailing attitude is that ironically paraphrased by Duff Cooper as, "There are only two religions: Roman Catholicism, which is wrong; and the rest, which don't matter." But what of a Catholic statesman? He believes that the truth is certainly known, and departures from it certainly (though not necessarily immediately) recognizable. It has been remarked earlier that the rejection of doctrinal indifferentism does not entail the rejection of religious freedom (nor the acceptance of the latter the acceptance of the former). Does this objection prove otherwise?

A simple reply lies to hand. It is never lawful to use unjust means, even in order to secure a good end or prevent a great evil; if it is true that the right to freedom of religion is a right in strict justice, then no purpose, however exalted, could justify its violation. This was the principle that St. Thomas used so firmly against the proposal to baptize the children of unbelievers against their parents' wishes. If the argument adduced in this chapter is sound, the objection is really answered.

But another reply is of interest to the student of political theory. Pope Pius XII rebutted the argument directly, that is, without invoking as a counter-argument the individual's rights in natural justice. Let us first quote the late Monsignor Knox's famous, and distressing, statement of the objection:

> Given such circumstances, is it certain that the Catholic Government of the nation would have no right to insist on Catholic education being universal (which is a form of coercion), and even to deport or imprison those who unsettled the mind of its subjects with new doctrines?

> It is certain that the Church would claim that right for the Catholic Government, even if considerations of prudence forbade its exercise in fact ... [He refers to the Catholic's certainty of the truth of his faith, and various threats to the convictions of simple people] ... And for those reasons a body of Catholic patriots, entrusted with the Government of a Catholic State, will not shrink even from repressive measures in order to perpetuate the

secure domination of Catholic principles among their fellow-countrymen.[1]

It is not only Catholics who have been shocked by this; people of other faiths have often recalled it as a *horrible exemplum*: if his Church's principles led Ronald Knox to talk like that, they are inclined to say, what can one expect from Catholics less gentle and far less enlightened than he? I have been told by some of his own friends that Knox, who was liable to consider that his lack of formal theological training counted against his own judgement, was persuaded (wrongly) that the view quoted above was an "official" view, enjoying at least extrinsic authority; but that subsequently he came to regret having submitted to over-persuasion. Whatever of such reports, one can imagine his pleasure at seeing Pope Pius XII deal with the objection in the allocution *Ci Riesce*.

This was an address which the Pope delivered to jurists in 1953, in which he discussed some of

[1] R. A. Knox, *The Belief of Catholics*, London, Ernest Benn, 1927, pp. 241–2. In later editions, Knox rewrote two of the sentences, complained that the passage had often been misleadingly quoted only in part or out of context, and asked that the latter version only be used. I have nevertheless ventured to put down the original here because it has often been cited as "the Catholic view"; as happened indeed, in one periodical at least, in an obituary note on Knox himself.

the problems to be expected in an international community of peoples. He studied the propriety of an arrangement whereby each member state, although making whatever regulations it chose concerning religious and moral affairs within its own borders, would none the less join in a common guarantee of freedom to each individual citizen (throughout the whole community of nations, and therefore in its own territory) to live according to his own religion or ethics; and, it is interesting to note, the Pope explicitly referred to the existence of many religious beliefs within a community. In particular, he dealt with a possible objection to the arrangement— the very objection based by Knox on the duty to repress evil whenever it lies within one's power—and rebutted it. The Pope put the objection as follows:

> The question is whether non-interference or toleration is permissible in some circumstances, and therefore positive repression not always a duty.[1]

He says that a glance at certain facts reveals the answer: it is in God's power to repress all error and moral deviation; yet his infinite perfection does not require him always to do so. He concludes:

[1] *AAS*, 45 (1953), p. 798.

Thus the affirmation that moral and religious deviation must always be hindered because tolerance is immoral is not absolutely and unconditionally valid.

The general phrasing of this is interesting. It is not merely that *the State* is not obliged to repress evil on all occasions when it is able to do so; *nobody* is under any such universal and unqualified obligation. We can therefore anticipate the corollary; the Pope continues:

Besides, God has not given to human authority any such absolute and universal command in the field either of faith or of morals. Such a command is unknown to the common convictions of mankind, to the Christian conscience, to the sources of revelation, and to the practice of the Church.

This deserves careful reading. Four possible bases have been considered for an argument to some universal duty or divine authorization to repress error whenever it lies in one's power, and all four are rejected. Applying these quite general principles, then, to the specific question of the State's alleged duty always to suppress religious or moral error, the Pope concludes:

Forbearance from the use of State laws and coercive measures can none the less be justified in the interests of a higher and more extensive good.

In this way, then, he answers the particular objection (based, that is, on the duty to repress evil) without invoking the individual's right, in strict justice, to freedom of conscience.

But another difficulty is raised at once. It is argued that, even though the Pope may have denied that it is always obligatory to repress evil, at least he implied that it is often right to do so. But this (it is objected) is incompatible with a thesis (such as mine) that a person has a strict right, as against the State, to do what his conscience dictates.

The point is an important one, and raises the question, Just what has the argument of this chapter proved? This question will reappear more sharply still at the end of the next major line of objection to be considered, and must be given a section to itself at the end of the chapter; at the moment it is enough to say this: I certainly do not want to deny, for instance, that the State is equally entitled to prevent the man who would murder on the plea of religion and the man who would murder for money. The British in India acted, not unjustly, but humanely, when they put down *suttee*. No account of freedom of conscience can be successful if it claims that a man has an absolute and unlimited right in all circumstances to do anything which he claims his religious principles demand; and the Pope was leaving no room for any such misconception. However, as the same need for some definition is called for once again in the next section of this chapter, it will be more conveniently left till then.

Another argument often adduced from the allocution *Ci Riesce* seems to be based on a misunderstanding. In setting out the principle that one is not always and necessarily obliged to repress evil whenever one can, the Pope remarked that forbearance may be justified, and even indeed be the better course of action, when it is practised "to further a greater good". Applying this to the question of civil toleration of religions, he said that this "can be justified in the interests of a higher and more general good". Now some people have wanted to interpret this, not as a matter of principle, but merely as a measure of expediency. The sort of meaning they would see as underlying it is, "If Protestant minorities are persecuted in Catholic countries, then Catholic minorities may suffer retaliation in Protestant lands; so we shall have to practise toleration as long as this danger exists."

This seems to me to misunderstand the Pope's argument. Throughout the address he is dealing with the propriety of joining an international community of nations in which religious pluralism would be recognized and protected. Some people had felt that, if Catholics joined such a community, they would be deserting their belief in the one true Church, condoning error,

and failing to repress evil. In reassuring such
people and disposing of their scruple, the Pope
constantly stresses the two aspects of a sound
solution. First, he is at pains to insist that error
is error and evil *is* evil; the Church will always
contest it by every talent of persuasion and
rhetoric and argument at her disposal, in season
and out of season. "Welcome or unwelcome,
bring home wrong-doing, comfort the waverer,
rebuke the sinner, with all the patience of a
teacher."[1] Sound principles concerning the
authority of conscience do not mean that we
should simply fold our arms and refrain from
all challenge of views we believe to be mistaken,
from all debate or controversy or exhortation.
But, second, the Pope is denying that one should
use *coercive* or *repressive* means to do so. St.
Paul's "patience of a teacher" is one thing;
Knox's "deportation or imprisonment" is quite
another.

Now the Pope points out that, as a general
moral principle, non-repression of evil may be
warranted "in the interests of a greater good";
and specifically with regard to State toleration
of religious and moral error, this "can be justified in the interests of a higher and more extensive good". This is important: not simply a more
extensive (*più vasto*) good, but also a higher one
(*superiore*). Perhaps the former qualification
might be satisfied by the explanation in terms

[1] 2 Tim. 4.2.

of expediency—namely, Catholic minorities will suffer if Catholic majorities repress: this might be a more extensive good; but it would not be a higher one. What would be such a higher good? One we have already seen: the freedom necessary to make a supernatural act of faith. This is the principal reason why the Church has always forbidden the use of force to compel people to enter her fold; but it is not the reason with which this essay is concerned. We have sought to establish another "higher good": *tranquillitas conscientiae*, the happy state of a good conscience, and so the freedom necessary to enjoy it by faithfully following one's conscientious convictions. It was a surprise to us earlier in our inquiry to find that St. Thomas nowhere made any connection between his principles concerning conscience and the question of religious freedom. Not so with Pope Pius XII; he explicitly cites respect for conscience as a reason for refraining from the use of *force majeure*, even when this lies in the power of Catholic statesmen:

> Out of respect for those who are in good conscience—mistaken indeed, but invincibly so—and of a different opinion, the Church has felt herself prompted to act, and has acted, along the lines of tolerance.[1]

[1] *AAS*, 45 (1953), p. 801.

One point of clarification needs to be stressed. It is not here claimed that the Pope, in *Ci Riesce*, spoke on the question studied in this chapter and gave the answer to which I have argued, namely, the individual's right to freedom of conscience. He was dealing with a separate though related question, namely, the problems in regard to religious freedom raised by an international community of sovereign states. What is claimed here is simply that he rejected this particular objection which has often been urged against the thesis of this essay: he denied that, in general, one is always obliged to prevent evil when it is in one's power to do so; and denied in particular that one is so obliged when religious error is in question.

2. "ERROR HAS NO RIGHTS"

The objection just considered, though new in its particular formulation, none the less has echoes of St. Thomas. But in recent times a new principle has been fashioned: "Error has no rights." This is often put forward as a self-evident principle which is literally true, and invoked as a major premiss for an argument against the case for the right to freedom of conscience; it establishes, says the objector, that no-one can have a right to practise any but the one religion founded by Christ. For the religious indifferentist, of course, this presents no difficulty; one religion is as good as another, he thinks, and no particular faith has any privileged claim to be true, or divinely founded. But the Catholic believes that there is only one Church established by Christ; is this, then, for him, an objection fatal to the claim that every man has the right to immunity from State interference with his religious freedom? I think not.

Against the objection, I want to argue first that the maxim, "Error has no rights", when taken literally, contains a logical fallacy; it is an example of a category mistake. It is almost sixty years since Lord Russell drew attention to the distinction between the range of truth and the range of significance of a term. In this connection Professor Ryle coined the phrase "category mistake". Mr. Manley Thompson has written a helpful study of how one may recognize category differences.[1] But for our present purpose we may simply take Ryle's definition: a category mistake is that logical fallacy committed by presenting facts which belong to one category in the idioms appropriate to another; or, more precisely, it consists in the allocation of concepts to logical types to which they do not belong.[2]

For a given *subject*, there is a range of predicates which may be meaningfully affirmed or

[1] *Philosophical Review*, Oct. 1957, p. 486.
[2] *The Concept of Mind*, London, Hutchinson, 1949, pp. 8, 17.

denied of it. But if we attribute to it a predicate lying outside that range, the result is not false, but meaningless; grammatically it may be a good sentence, but logically it is not a proposition at all. For example, to the subject "John Doe" we may appropriately ascribe predicates such as the following: free, or slave; white, or coloured; twenty-one, or under twenty-one. Some of the resultant propositions would be true and some would be false, but all would be meaningful. This is not the case with predicates such as the following: rhyming, or blank-verse; steam-driven, or oil-burning; analytic, or synthetic; fixed, or planetary. The resultant propositions would be neither true nor false; these predicates apply only to subjects which are members of categories to which the term "John Doe" does not belong. Likewise, for a given *predicate*, there is a range of subjects to which it may be meaningfully ascribed, but if it is applied to a subject beyond this range, the result is not false but meaningless. For example, the predicate "having wheels" may be affirmed or denied of such subjects as motor-cars, aircraft or clocks; but not of overcoats, jokes or sonatas. Such inappropriate predications do not constitute propositions at all, and the logical fallacy committed in attempting to make them is conveniently called a category mistake.

Now, this is precisely the mistake present in

the dictum, "Error has no rights", when it is literally understood. The predicate *"having rights"*, in its literal acceptance, is properly attributed *only to persons*. Thus Genicot, as we have seen, defines a right as "the moral power *of a person* to have or to do something", etc. We saw, too, that Delos' study showed that a right arises from the different relationships two persons bear to a common object, and led to the following definition:

A right is a complex whole comprising two persons and an object, the persons being joined by a relation of which the object is the term which both unites them and determines the character of the relationship.

It seems clear enough, then, that the predicate "having rights" is properly attributed *only to persons*. This may apply to individual persons, or to groups of them—that is, corporate persons such as joint-stock companies, sporting bodies, political parties, national states, religious societies or "churches". But it cannot be meaningfully predicated of propositions, theories, arguments or doctrines; for a right is an arrangement between persons, a relationship between them with regard to some object. This object, of course, may be a theory or a doctrine, though more commonly it is an inanimate possession or a proposed course of action. We could quite properly argue whether or not a professor of surgery had or had not any right to teach a controverted method of frontal lobotomy; but we could not properly argue whether or not the method had any right to be taught. The sentence "Error has no rights", then, if it be taken strictly as it stands, is neither true nor false; it is meaningless; it is an instance of a category mistake. Although for grammatical purposes it is a sentence in correct form, in logic it is not a proposition at all. In its literal acceptance it is in no better logical case than the sentence, "Error has no wheels".

Supposing now we take the dictum in some non-literal acceptances. It is a familiar linguistic fact that we often find it convenient to use shorthand summaries of important principles and phrases. No harm is done, provided we remember that they *are* shorthand, and not to be taken as literally true. The title of this book is a case in point; literally speaking, conscience has no rights: only persons have rights; but the phrase, "the rights of conscience", is a useful shorthand for, "A person's rights with regard to the dictates of his conscience." The question is, then: Can the sentence, "Error has no rights", be translated into some logically proper proposition which tells as an objection against our thesis?

The dictum is sometimes expanded into the

proposition, "A man who is in error has no right
to (believe or act upon) his error." Such a version
is in sound logical form; it is a genuine proposition which contains no category mistake or other
logical fallacy. But it is not an argument; it is
simply a statement that the opposite view is
mistaken. If it were the conclusion of a syllogism
it would indeed tell directly against the position
reached in the present chapter; but to do so
effectively it would first need a major and a
minor premiss to establish it. That a man who
is in error has no right to his error *as such* is
clear enough; but what the objector has to dis-
prove is that the man has a right to a belief,
or an action, or an omission, in so far as it is
necessary for him to honour his obligations as
presented to him by his conscience. A simple
statement to the opposite effect does not constitute an objection.

A more formidable expansion goes somewhat
as follows: the sentence, "Error has no rights",
is merely a compendious way of saying, "No-one
has a right to do what is wrong." This looks
much more serious. It is a genuine proposition,
in correct logical form; it tells against the alleged
claim of a right to freedom of conscience; and it
can be supported by argument somewhat as follows: "You seek to derive the right to do X from
the presence of a moral obligation to do X. But
one cannot have a moral obligation to do what

is wrong: for that would be tantamount to saying, X is both morally obligatory and morally wrong. Therefore one cannot have a right to do what is wrong."

To meet the objection one would point to the ambiguity latent in the term "moral obligation". Rights are derived, not immediately from what is *objectively* of moral obligation, but from what is subjectively so. For ultimately, rights are derived from and accounted for in terms of *ends and needs*; in so far as X is necessary for a person to attain his end, the sovereign end of personal existence, he has a right to X. Now, substantial fidelity to one's personal moral obligations is a necessary means to attaining one's end; this refers to what is *subjectively* one's obligation; and this in turn refers to that which one's conscience dictates: "An erroneous conscience is binding in exactly the same way as is a correct one, and an action will have in fact whatever goodness or evil conscience attributes to it." So this version of the dictum breaks down through an ambiguity in its use of the word "wrong"; it fails to distinguish between what is objectively wrong or materially sinful, and what is subjectively wrong or formally sinful. Rights in the strict sense can be only subjective rights, and hence cannot be finally settled in terms of objective norms.

Let us see, finally, the statement used by Pope

Pius XII when he wanted to use a condensed form of the relevant principle. He wrote:

> Whatever is at odds with truth and the moral law has objectively no right to existence, propagation or action.[1]

The Pope did not use the phrase "objective right", as one otherwise excellent English translation rendered him at this point; strictly speaking, a right is something essentially subjective and personal, as we have found; his phrase was, "has objectively no right to existence". If it is asked, "What right has A to say X?" the answer, "X is true," will often be sufficient; the answer, "X is false", plainly will not, and a right in its regard will have to be vindicated on other grounds.

Objectively, one always has the duty to accept and respect whatever is true and morally sound; and on objective grounds there is no such duty to respect something which is at odds with truth or the moral law. But the fact that some person, through a mistaken conscience, judges it to be his duty introduces a new element. Another man has no duty immediately with regard to the erroneous *view* itself, but to the *person* who mistakenly accepts it and does have a personal and subjective duty in its regard. When there is question of religious bodies, there is, of course,

[1] *AAS*, 45 (1953), p. 798.

a profound point behind the Pope's statement. We have already noticed that rights may belong to corporate persons as well as to individuals; typical and important instances are religious bodies. Now, the Catholic believes that his Church's right to existence, propagation and action arises *objectively* from its historic institution and empowerment by Christ and the divine authority with which he still rules it through his vicar; to violate its rights is, in a real sense, to commit an injustice against God. The rights of other religious bodies have a different origin. It is not that they arise by grant or recognition of the State, as might be held, say, by T. H. Green's social convention theory of rights. They arise *subjectively,* out of the need their members have to meet their subjective, personal obligations by following the dictates of their conscience. Here again Genicot's principles are relevant: "An erroneous conscience, provided it be certain, shows a man what is God's will for him in exactly the same way as does a correct one."[1]

Those who do not share our faith will see the

[1] *Institutiones Theologiae Moralis*, Brussels, Desclée, 1931, vol. 1, p. 42. This must not be understood as an opinion on the separate, difficult question of "salvation outside the Church". Substantial fidelity to moral duty is a necessary, but not a sufficient, condition of salvation. Different theologians hold very different opinions as to what constitute the sufficient conditions.

point that is being made, but will not agree with it. It may therefore be interesting to see that a rather similar point is made by a non-Christian liberal philosopher. It occurs in Dr. McCloskey's interesting study of this and related questions:

> "Error and evil have no rights" is, in general, an accurate statement of the case, that there are no abstract rights to evil as there are to goods—such as virtue, knowledge, and goods such as happiness.[1]

His phrase "no abstract rights" is not quite so happily chosen, perhaps, as the Pope's "has, objectively, no right to existence"; it seems to suggest the odd implication that an abstract right is more valuable and more stringent than a concrete one. But his account shows that the dictum in question can be expanded (though not literally translated) into a meaningful proposition which is not, of course, a self-evident initial premiss, but an important conclusion. Does such a conclusion undermine the thesis of this book?

This is not the place to study McCloskey's argument in detail. His metaphysical assumptions are very different from those of this chapter, and the basis of his defence of freedom accordingly different too:

[1] H. J. McCloskey, "The State and Evil", in *Ethics*, University of Chicago, April 1959, p. 184.

Where it cannot be known *with reasonable assurance* what is really obligatory and really good, the abstract right may give rise to a derivative right to act in accordance with one's beliefs.[1]

On this account, the right to religious freedom would be based on religious agnosticism or indifferentism, which I should be at pains to reject. Furthermore, his analysis of right is not in terms of a teleological account of the many-faceted end of man, but in terms of what is intrinsically obligatory. Such things cannot be argued here. But one strikingly phrased conclusion of McClosky leads to a last question:

The man who believes that life is evil or that people should be put out of their misery and who acts accordingly has no more of a claim to an abstract right to kill than has the person who rightly believes that the taking of a life of an innocent person against his wishes is wrong.

This seems incontestably true. Does it contradict the thesis I have tried to prove?

3. The Limits of the Argument

This essay has argued towards a single conclusion: that a person has a right to follow his

[1] McCloskey, p. 185.

conscience, with freedom from State interference, in matters of religious choice, profession and worship. But what does this mean in practice? Let me say at once that a detailed answer lies beyond the present terms of reference, and would need to incorporate the advice of the political scientist and the constitutional lawyer. Nevertheless something must be said of the sense in which the right to freedom of conscience is here being asserted. Is it maintained that a man has an absolute and unlimited right to do anything which he claims his religious beliefs demand? If so, it will make things decidedly awkward. Surely the State is empowered to prevent the community from religious charlatans, from cranks, and from vicious social practices. If not, we should have to revise many of our ordinary opinions, and condemn many interventions of authority which are usually accepted as permissible or even admirable.

The Jewish prophets set their face against the old Semitic practice of slaying first-born children in sacrifice; various aberrations of religion had led many of the Hebrews to take up the practice, often in nightmarish forms, and the prophets claimed divine authority to put the horror down. Pope Clement VI and the Emperor Charles IV, as well as the Sorbonne at Paris, worked together to prohibit flagellation-pilgrimages, and the many acts of violence and perversion which the brotherhood of the Flagellants practised in the name of union with Christ's redemptive sufferings. The British in India succeeded in abolishing the Hindu rite of *suttee*, which required a widow to throw herself on her husband's funeral pyre. In the 1830's Lord William Bentinck's Government succeeded in putting down the Thagi, or Thugs, a sect which, for about seven hundred years, had strangled and looted in the name of their religious beliefs. They claimed that the goddess Kali had commanded them to strangle and rob, and the scholar and soldier who put an end to the practice declared that no thug ever felt the slightest compunction for his crimes. He wrote:

> A thug considers the persons murdered precisely in the light of victims offered up to the Goddess. He meditates his murders without any misgivings, he perpetrates them without any emotions of pity, and he remembers them without any feelings of remorse.[1]

Any theory which claimed immunity for people to practise such rites in the name of freedom of religious conscience would be nonsense. All serious moral discussion is in terms of the morally normal and adult responsible human

[1] W. H. Sleeman, *Ramaseena*, quoted in the *Encyclopaedia of Religion and Ethics*, Edinburgh, Clark, 1921, vol. 12, p. 260.

being; but people who make demands like these are moral monsters.[1] There can be depravity through debased social custom as well as through personal fault, as St. Thomas reminds us,[2] and the assessment of personal responsibility and guilt in the individual who inherits such customs is not our business; but the custom followed by the moral monster does not create rights such that the normal human being must submit to them or the State protect them. Of course, one must use sober language in such discussion, and be slow to style those with whose moral views we differ as "monsters". When I hear of the abortionist who uses craniotomy I am inclined to say, "Only an inhuman monster would cold-bloodedly crush a baby's head"; but there are cases when people with other views would say of mine, "Only a monster would sit back and let the mother of a family die when he could do the one thing necessary to save her." However, these are simply the first emotional reactions of sharp moral disagreement. We can explain our position, each to the other, and debate and argue the points on which we differ. With the human-sacrificer and the ritual-killer, however, argument is useless and legal restraint does not seem improper. Earlier in this essay we

[1] The phrase was suggested by Dr. A. C. Jackson, in private discussion.
[2] *ST*, 1–2,94,4c.

found with regret that we could not draw up a complete list of the primary precepts of the natural law, and here there is similar difficulty; but the term "moral monster" has a recognizable application, if not a definable scope, and where there is good faith it can be safely embodied in and enforced by law. Where there is not good faith any law can be monstrously interpreted.

But the extreme cases of savagery raise a more practical point. The right to freedom of religion is only one of the many rights which a really human community must protect. Now it is a familiar fact of social experience that our rights are tempered by the rights of others. In some cases these "others" will be other indivduals; the first man to arrive in the doctor's surgery has a right to be seen before later arrivals, but he may have to yield to a haemorrhage case rushed in later still. In other cases my rights are tempered by the demands of the common good; the individual's right to freedom is quite properly limited in war-time, and his right to property legitimately curtailed by taxation in time of peace. Of some rights we say quite bluntly that they must be subordinated to others. But of some rights this is not so; they are so intimately related to the individual's attaining his end that to subordinate them would be tantamount to subordinating his end to some other human value; whereas the individual end is a sovereign good.

Such rights may be co-ordinated with those of others, but never subordinated to them. Thus a typical democratic constitution both guarantees respect for the individual's right to religious freedom and adverts to the need for its co-ordination with the rights of others:

> Freedom of conscience, and the free profession and practice of religion are, subject to public order and morality, guaranteed to every citizen.[1]

This is to come to the limits of our terms of reference, to the threshold of constitutional law and political science; but there is one point which the theorist may yet put before the experts in these more practical disciplines. Though the State is not competent to decide what is true and what is false in questions of religion, it may have to decide whether a given belief or set of beliefs is properly described as religious. In a famous hearing before the Australian High Court it was claimed that a person who objected to compulsory military training on religious grounds could not, because of Section 116 of the Constitution, be validly compelled to undergo such training. The High Court rejected the claim, holding that this section excluded only laws which would prohibit the practice of religion. It said:

[1] Constitution of Éire, art. 44. 2 (i).

To require a man to do a thing which has nothing at all to do with religion is not prohibiting him from a free exercise of religion.[1]

My point is not whether the argument for freedom of conscience, when carried a step beyond my own objective, protects the moral principles involved by membership of a certain Church or religious body; the sole conclusion of this essay concerns freedom of religious choice, profession and worship. My point is that the right to religious freedom must be definable and testable by law. To deny this is to say that a person has a right to do anything at all, provided he calls it an exercise of religion. May it not happen, then, that a court, with the utmost sincerity and the best will in the world, may rule that a given act does not constitute a genuine exercise of religion when, in fact, the defendant sincerely believes that it does? May this not lead to the State's withholding from him the one thing necessary for the integrity of his conscience, whose rights may be subordinated to no other good?

This raises a delicate point, which is true enough, but dangerous. Strictly speaking, very strictly indeed, my argument might be said to

[1] Krygger v. Williams, 15 C.L.R. 366 at 369: quoted by J. R. Kerr, "Freedom under the Law", in "Freedom of Belief", published in *Manna*, Sydney, 1958, p. 72.

prove only the right to *interior* freedom, freedom of the internal act of the will itself. It is on that alone that the individual's moral performance is judged. Think, for instance, of the person who unwittingly reveals a secret under truth-drugs, the priest who fails to attend a dying parishioner because he himself is in a political prison, the woman whose chastity is violated by force against her will; none of these people incurs moral guilt. In this sense the State simply *cannot* violate the right to freedom of conscience; no matter what it does, the human will is in principle never constrained to act against the dictates of conscience. Where there is no freedom there is no responsibility or blame; heroic virtue will not be conquered by dungeon, fire or sword. But as a basis for practice, this is nonsense. Only the tiniest fraction of people are heroes. The fact is that, given State pressure, many people will conform, reluctantly and regretfully perhaps, but responsibly; without freedom of religion guaranteed and protected by the State, they will yield to pressure and compromise conscience, and stand in real danger of moral and spiritual ruin. Even economic pressure will often be sufficient for this; hence the safeguards forbidding any particular religious profession as a qualification for public office, laid down in the constitutions which we have quoted. It is therefore quite correct to say that the State acts unjustly when its actions lead to a person's acting against conscience in the relevant sense: the more so since the powers it holds have been given to help people attain their end. It is on reasons such as this that one might argue a case (on grounds of moral principle) for the points made by the High Court (on constitutional grounds) in another case involving Section 116: that the section protects not only opinions, but also acts, and that the word "religion" extends not only to internal belief, but to worship and the practices and observances of religion.[1] This is because the normal effect of State action will often induce reactions endorsed by the will itself.

None the less, there is a point here. Strictly speaking, the immediate action of the State terminates far short of the will. There could be cases where it might lawfully foresee and permit, though never intend, that the restraining of certain actions would be felt at the level of conscience and will. The argument here is parallel to that concerning the right to life. Less stringent rights than that to life and freedom of conscience may be directly subordinated to the common good: but these two, never. It is never lawful, in any circumstances, directly to kill an innocent man. None the less, the State may introduce compulsory military service. It

---

[1] The case concerned the Jehovah's Witnesses, and Kerr quotes from 67 C.L.R. 116: *Manna*, p. 72.

foresees and permits that this may lead to the death of many innocent citizens. This is justified, because three conditions are fulfilled. First, the good which the State is protecting is of comparable value to the good, the right to which it is allowing to be jeopardized: the lives of the citizens. Second, its direct intention does not terminate at the evil in question (the innocent man's death) but at the good it needs (his service under arms). Third, the evil effect it foresees as possible—the conscript's death—is not a means necessary for the attainment of its objective, the nation's safety; it is a by-product of what it does directly intend, his service under arms. If any of these conditions were violated, the proposed measure could not be justified.

Much more rarely, there may be parallel cases justified with regard to conscience. A person claims that a certain action is part of his religious practice; the State sees that it will be gravely subversive of public order. It therefore proposes to restrain the person's external action, though making no attempt to constrain his internal beliefs. Are any of the three relevant conditions violated? The State's direct intention does not terminate at the evil in question (the will's failure to follow conscience) but at the good sought (the preservation of public order). The possible evil is in no way a means necessary to this good; the good would be procured in exactly the same way, whatever the internal state of the person affected. However, the third condition will be rarely possible of fulfilment. Since the good jeopardized by the proposed State interference is at the level of moral and spiritual integrity, the good jeopardized by State non-interference would have to be of a like order; we are reminded of Pius XII's earlier consideration of a "higher and more extensive good"; how extremely unusual it would be for such an argument to be applicable is suggested by these words of the Chief Justice in the case mentioned:

> It is consistent with the maintenance of religious freedom for the State to restrain actions and courses of conduct which are inconsistent with the maintenance of civil government or prejudicial to the continued existence of the community. The Constitution protects religion within a community organized under a Constitution, so that continuance of such protection necessarily assumes continuance of the community so organised.[1]

Such cases will be desperately rare; and only such cases can warrant the invocation of this argument. The sort of faith that might lawfully be denied the protection of organized society is that which acts on the belief that organized

[1] Kerr, p. 73.

society is essentially evil, and hence jeopardizes the freedom of others' consciences.

The "Argument from the Thin End of the Wedge" is always rightly viewed with suspicion, and here surely is the paradigm case of it. For one thing, there is the theoretical problem of giving a coherent account of indirect intention, of the distinction between the effect we directly intend and the effect we foresee and permit, but do not directly intend. There is also the practical danger that a person will sooner or later conform his interior act of the will to the external action forced upon him, and of the spiritual ruin to which this may well lead. Consequently there is required the very gravest of reasons to invoke the argument; the most serious onus of proof lies upon the State before it may appeal to it, and a healthy community will be most sceptical about the presence of the necessary conditions. Still, the possibility does exist, the law must provide for it, and one must hope for judges of the highest integrity to hear the rare case that may arise. Further than this one can hardly go without trespassing on the domain of the constitutional lawyer.

Other questions must be left to the political scientist. For instance, it will often be for him to judge whether the right to freedom of conscience is viable in a given situation. "There can be no right to the impossible", says Father Burn-heim:

> Where it is possible for the individual to reach a personal and reasoned conviction on religious matters he has a clear right to do so, and with modern facilities of education and communications these conditions do exist, and the right cannot be withheld. On the other hand, in a society where most people are illiterate, communications undeveloped, and where the conditions for rational decision are not present, then it is infinitely better that these people be protected from error than that they be abandoned to irrational forces in the name of a freedom they are not in a position to exercise.[1]

Much hasty criticism of the Church's action in many historical situations has come from overlooking this point. It is in terms such as this that some people believe that a case might be made out to justify some colonial powers' curtailing the full freedom of missionary activity in primitive territories, as when specified areas are assigned to the different denominations to prevent inter-tribal religious strife. It is one thing to say that the Church refrains from urging her right (which she certainly never loses) to "preach the Gospel to every creature" in the interests of

[1] J. Burnheim, in the same issue of *Manna*, p. 79.

avoiding bloodshed which would do more harm than good to the missionary cause; but what of the right of every individual native throughout the region to hear the truth? Perhaps an answer is to be given in terms such as these: the conditions do not yet exist for providing, and enjoying, adult liberties in what is still a primitive, morally non-adult community. A cautious parallel is to be drawn with the rights of parents in regard to their children; before the child has reached the age of full moral responsibility he cannot plead against his parents the right to be allowed to join any religious group to which he is childishly attracted. It is possible that the sincere application of the parallel may occasionally justify a quite healthy paternalism, with the State *in loco parentis*. Once again, we should be slow to believe that the conditions for full freedom are not present, and the case for paternalism warranted. People who have held power relinquish it with reluctance, and can easily delude themselves that only they "know what is best for these natives". Here one can but acknowledge that the argument can conceivably be valid on occasions, and warn of the danger of its being abused. The decision that it is or is not applicable may belong to experts in more practical disciplines. This is as far as the present discussion can go.

For this essay has set itself a limited objective. From a whole skein of related questions it sought to unravel a single thread: the right to freedom of religious conscience. No synthesis has been attempted of relations between Church and State. No analysis has been made of the origin of the powers or the extent of the competencies of these two institutions. There has been no investigation of the propriety of an Established Church or a Confessional State. No points of dogmatic theology have been considered—the question of salvation for those outside the Church; her authority and use of spiritual sanctions over her own members; her right to speak on moral issues, even when they have application in domestic, business or political life. Two conclusions only have been argued: the obligation to follow one's conscience when it has been formed in good faith; and the right to follow it, with freedom from State interference, in matters of religious faith, profession and worship. Compared with the great issues left untouched, these are small enough conclusions. But I believe that they are true.

POSTSCRIPT

"WERE it proper in such a subject", wrote Hume at the end of the *Treatise*, "to bribe the reader's assent, or employ anything but solid argument, we are here abundantly supplied with topics to engage the affections"; and the present much more modest project may well end on a similar note. This essay has argued that religious freedom is demanded by sound *principles*; another book could be written to show that its effective guarantee is also the best *policy*.

The Church's mission extends to all men, and is not confined to those who are already her members. She can never think of those who do not belong to her as an enemy to be watched with suspicion or hostility. Pope Pius XII voiced the Church's anxiety that those outside her family be rescued from "a state in which they cannot be certain of their salvation", and her longing to welcome them "as children coming back to their own father's home." It was natural, then, that he should stipulate that it is absolutely necessary for this to come about by the perfectly free choice of those concerned, with no shadow of force or constraint. Not merely would the use of force or constraint be evil and wrong, he says; it would be useless: for such people would not become real believers at all: "That faith, without which 'it is impossible to please God', must be the perfectly free 'homage of intellect and will.'"[1] So it is always an important part of the Church's mission to win the glad and affectionate allegiance of those outside her.

How is this to be done? Certainly not by any display of harshness or pressure or force. St. Paul's advice was to preach and comfort and exhort "with all the patience of a teacher"[2]; and as a matter of sheer good tactics we must admire the way that Pope Gregory the Great faithfully echoed St. Paul's advice: "If it is a person's sincere intention to lead those outside the Christian religion to the true faith, he must take persuasive measures rather than harsh ones; for *minds that might well be attracted to the truth by a reasoned statement of our case will simply be alienated by hostility.*"

It would be a pity to create a false impression here. I do not mean that one should forbear from the use of force merely as a matter of expediency; the argument of this essay has been that the right to religious freedom is a matter of strict principle. My point here is simply to suggest

[1] Encyclical *Mystici Corporis*, London, Catholic Truth Society, p. 62.
[2] 2 Tim, 4.2.

that what is right in principle is also best in practice. There is one thing necessary if the Church is to win those outside her: that the face she presents to the world should be known for the face of Christ.

On the one hand, therefore, the Church can never appear tentative or indecisive, palely anxious to make a good impression, eager to please; ready to water down her principles lest some of her children walk with her no more. Nobody would recognize Christ in a Church like that. But on the other hand, she would never persuade the stranger that she was the Church of Christ if she led him to see behind her "a God of prey, whose sole purpose is to subjugate and enslave", as Gabriel Marcel has put it. It is not merely that an acid test of a genuine democracy is the way it treats minorities; there is a Christian principle at stake, a principle given us in the Gospel itself: "As you would have men treat you, you are to treat them; not otherwise." Pope Gregory IX applied this rigorously to the way Christian states should treat Jewish minorities; he said, "Christians must show to Jews that same forbearance which we should like to have shown to Christians in pagan lands." Any other behaviour will convince people that, whatever else may be the basis of our policy, it is certainly not the Sermon on the Mount. It is the mark of a Christian priest that he gives aid and comfort to

the person who is in ignorance and error; and it
is the mark of a Christian people that they deal
gently with groups whom they believe to be in
ignorance and error. In this way they may be
recognized as followers of Christ; not otherwise.

Mary Tudor was not a saint; and, although
she "meant well", her methods have led long
generations to distrust and hate the Church she
intended to serve. Pope Gregory the Great was a
saint; and his policy was very different. The Jewish community at Naples had complained to him
that a law was soon to be made to end their
ancient freedom of worship. The Pope wrote to
the Bishop of Naples the letter from which I
have just quoted, charging him to see that no
such disabilities were imposed. His advice was
not only more saintly, but immortally more
effective:

If it is a person's sincere intention to lead
those outside the Christian religion to the true
faith, he must take persuasive measures rather
than harsh ones; for minds that might well be
attracted to the truth by a reasoned statement
of our case will simply be alienated by hostility. If he pleads some such "sincere intention" as his excuse for acting otherwise, and
putting an end to the customary Jewish worship, he stands revealed as seeking his own
ends rather than God's . . . What is the point

of abolishing a freedom which these people have long enjoyed, when such action would do nothing to help their conversion to the Faith? Why dictate to Jewish people about their religious practices if this makes it impossible for us to win them? Our line of action should be by way of reason, and kindness; to make them want to follow us, not flee from us; to point to their own Scriptures for the evidence of what we say: and in this way, with God's help, to convert them to the Church, our mother.[1]

What is right in principle is also best in practice.

[1] *Epist. XIII* (*Ad Paschasium, Episc. Neapol.*), 12. (*PL*, 77,1267.)